S C A R E   M E

BY JOSH RUBEN

SCARE ME

by

Josh Ruben

Producers
Alex Bach, Daniel Powell,
& Josh Ruben

Co-Producers
Eamon Downey
& Brendan H.Banks

Executive Producers
Philip Erodes, David Kiger,
Steven Stodghill, Brian Steinberg,
& Tucker Voorhees

Co-Executive Producers
Michael Bulger, Danny Dykowsky,
& Christine Nangle

Cinematography
Brendan H. Banks

Cover Art and Booklet Design
Henry Gonzalez

SCARE ME

Written by

Josh Ruben

INT. CAR - AFTERNOON

A Catskills cabbie - BETTINA - yaps to FRED, nursing a migraine in the back.

BETTINA
You're a writer?

Bettina doesn't see Fred nod with her eyes on the road.

BETTINA (CONT'D)
You're a writer, or??

FRED
Yes. Well, actor. Writer. Director-

BETTINA
TRIPLE THREAT! Been in anything I seen!?

Fred shakes his head "no."

FRED
Yeah. I work at an ad agency. (under his breath) *And I wanna kill myself.*

BETTINA
Sorry to bother ya by the way! I know ya just got off a flight from Europe or whatever.

FRED
LA.

BETTINA
Please feel free to tell me to "shush." But, I just love talking to people. S'why I do the job, y'know. Some people get in the cab and they're just like *"DON'T TALK TO ME!"* and it's like,*"Suit your fuckin' self!"*

She laughs too much.

Finally, silence.

Fred leans his head back and closes his ey-

BETTINA (CONT'D)
Feel free to take a nap, or anything! You must be tired.

FRED
Thanks.

BETTINA
I do some writing myself.

Jesus.

FRED
Oh, do you.

He LOOKS OUT THE WINDOW - pathetic, passing landscapes. A gas station. A desolate orchard. Tarps in yards.

BETTINA
Sure. I made some bad decisions in my life, y'know? Bad investments and such. Like, *"WHY WOULD YOU DO THAT."* But I gotta say: never had more joy than writin' a movie. I like that whole *"process."* Wrote it with a buddy of mine. Well. My ex. Screwed me over, actually. We don't talk no more, so.

FRED
Yeah, it's uh. Writing is, uh.

Fred gets a TEXT MESSAGE. He reads it, jaw clenched.

BETTINA
Best idea though I ever had, though? Honestly, James Cameron could do it.

Bettina pronounces it *"Camera-On."*

FRED
Oh, wow?

BETTINA
Uh huh. I can't tell ya much about it - writer code and all? But I will say without a uh, unquestionably, it'd make millions. But it's the story of Korah? The story of Korah? He rallied a mob against Moses, but God intervenes and all hell breaks loose? Could be one of those movies James Camera-on could do.

FRED
You mentioned that, yeah. That's exciting, uh-

BETTINA
Bettina.

FRED
Oh yeah no, I wasn't asking your name. You just passed it-

BETTINA
Oh FUCK, SORRY!

Bettina STOMPS ON THE BRAKES.

2 EXT. FRED'S CABIN - AFTERNOON 2

Bettina's RUSTED MERCURY SABLE (or similar) *180s*, growling toward a small, rustic house.

BETTINA (V.O.)
Hard to see up here with all the woods and all.

FRED (V.O.)
Uh huh.

3 EXT. CAR - CONTINUOUS 3

They roll up to Fred's CABIN. It's rustic and has a decent little patio. A babbling BROOK cuts through the backyard.

Bettina parks, opens the trunk and pulls out Fred's ROLLER SUITCASE, immediately dropping it in the dirt.

BETTINA
Oh shit- er. CRAP. Sorry. I got it!

FRED
No. I got it. You're good.

BETTINA
Looks like a haunted house! Beware POLTERGEISTS! And stuff.

She pulls out a GROCERY BAG from the backseat.

FRED
Will do.

BETTINA
Just beer, huh?

He takes the bag and hands her CASH.

FRED
I don't have a tip. Sorry.

BETTINA
Honestly, the conversation was a tip in and of itself.

Fred starts toward the house.

BETTINA (CONT'D)
And if you need any recommendations for what to do in town or heck, wanna beer buddy-

FRED
Just gonna be doing some work. Alone. Thanks.

BETTINA
Writer code.

FRED
Sure. Bye. Bettina.

BETTINA
Goodnight to you too, Mr. Banks! Do you go by Fred or Mr. Banks?

HOLD ON: Bettina. We HEAR Fred SHUT THE DOOR.

BETTINA (CONT'D)
Do you go by Fred or Mr. Banks?

She does a smiley *"Nevermind wave"* and gets in her car.

WIDE - Bettina pulls out of the driveway.

This is the first time we see the cabin in all its peculiar, rustic glory.

4 INT. FRED'S CABIN - AFTERNOON 4

INSERT (FOOT LEVEL) - Fred drops his bag.

INSERT - Fred lifts his LAPTOP into frame.

INSERT - He cracks open a BEER.

MED - Fred sits, in for a night of writing.

LAPTOP SCREEN: ***WEREWOLF IDEAS. Good if he has guns? revenge***

BEHIND FRED'S HEAD - Fred does a long, weird stretch.

VARIOUS MOMENTS of Fred doing anything *but* writing:

- Fred picks his nose and eats a booger.

- Fred looks in the bathroom mirror and hisses like a cat.

- WE FOLLOW Fred walk around the sun-basked living room.

- Fred traces his fingers along the HEARTH then looks up.

- WIDE - Fred eyes a massive TAXIDERMY mounted to the wall above the fireplace.

- GLIDE toward a KNIFE BLOCK on the KITCHEN COUNTER. Fred's hand ENTERS FRAME, tracing his fingers along the handles.

- MED - BEHIND FRED'S HEAD - He raises a KNIFE, making *"Psycho" SLASH* sounds, before receiving a TEXT. He picks up his phone and puts it down, flustered.

- Fred screams ***YES!*** as if stoked to be... single.

- MED - Fred gets another TEXT. He picks it up, reads, then pushes it into the cushions of the couch. We don't see his face until he buries it face into a pillow and screams.

AT THE DESK

Fred returns to his computer. He searches *THE STORY OF KORAH.*

CUT TO:

5 INT. FRED'S CABIN - NIGHT 5

TOP SHOT - Fred takes the last bite of a pathetic TV DINNER.

Something catches his eye. He looks **right at us.**

REVERSE: TRUCK-IN toward THE CELLAR DOOR.

TRUCK-IN toward Fred. He makes subtle *"footstep"* sounds out of the side of his mouth.

He narrates to himself in a quiet, creepy rasp:

FRED
Let me ouuuut. Let me ouuuuuuut.

BANG! Fred jumps.

FRED (CONT'D)
...hello?

Probably just the house.

FRED APPROACHES THE CELLAR DOOR, walking INTO FOCUS, and turns the KNOB.

POV STAIRWELL - Fred's silhouette feels very *CREEP.*

FRED (CONT'D)
Nope.

An INSIDIOUS TONE swells to an ORCHESTRAL STING!

CUT TO:

6 EXT. COOPER LAKE ROAD - THE NEXT MORNING 6

The MUSIC TRANSITIONS to *Gonna Get Along Without You Now* by Skeeter Davis (or something similarly cheery) over INSERTS:

- GREY CLOUDS ROLL above a creepy CHURCH

- BRANCHES careening

- The deranged FACE of an eroding LAWN ORNAMENT

SUPER WIDE - An ant-sized FRED jogs through frame. If we look closely, we can see ANOTHER JOGGER pass him.

ON THE ROAD - we FOLLOW FRED (*Wrestler*-style) - the music now a tinny murmur from his HEADPHONES.

Just ahead is the JOGGER from before (if you could identify the colors) now sitting on a GUARD RAIL, clutching her knee with one EAR BUD in.

WIDE PUSH-IN:

FRED
Hi.

WOMAN
Hi.

FRED
Knee?

WOMAN
Knee.

WOMAN (CONT'D)
It's okay, you don't need to make small talk. You're clearly winded.

SHOT / REV SHOT - on FRED's CU first:

FRED
Nope, definitely not trying to uh, do that, but. Need anything? I can get some ice or- I'm in the cabin just down that driveway.

WOMAN
Huh. I'm in a cabin down *that* driveway.

FRED
Huh. Fred.

WOMAN
Oh, I wasn't asking for your name, but...

FRED
Ah. Sorry. I am Fred. Though.

FANNY
I'm kidding. I'm not a dick. Fanny.

FRED
You're not a "dick Fanny"?

FANNY
I mean. I *am* a dick Fanny, but my name is also "Fanny."

FRED
That's fun. I know a couple with a dog named Franny.

FANNY
Cool! So again, I'm "Fanny" which isn't the same, because, no 'R'. Fanny. Like a bum. *"Don't slap my fanny!"* Do you understand?

FRED
I understand. I didn't mean to offend you.

FANNY
You can't offend me. I'm a sociopath.

FRED
A female sociopath?

FANNY
Women can be sociopaths.

FRED
I know.

FANNY
Well I'm gonna walk back this way. *Limp.*

FRED
Yeah, I'm headed, uh-

They re-enter a TRACKING TWO-SHOT as they walk up the road:

FANNY
So, what are you running from?

FRED
Running? Not running. I'm writing.

FANNY
So am I. Drove up from the city? Hashtag "Escape Brooklyn"?

FRED
LA, actually. I flew in yesterday and leave tomorrow, believe it or not.

FANNY
That's the stupidest thing I've ever heard.

FRED
Well not back to LA, but, somewhere. Yeah. So, you're a writer?

FANNY
Yeah. Novelist. Horror. Why.

FRED
So do I.

FANNY
So do you? As in "so you novel, too?" Anything I've read?

FRED
Oh, I've got a few things, in uh. I've had a few things in development. I'm in advertising. I'm putting my focus *back* on just writing. More. Like you. How about you? Have you written anything I've read?

FANNY
You could've just said "No" but, uh, yeah, I wrote a book called "Venus." It's about a boy and his-

FRED
Mother and the zombie outbreak that affects only women. I know Venus. You wrote "Venus"? No you didn't.

FANNY
I'm a sociopath. I'm not a liar.

FRED
You wrote Venus! I heard about it on Fresh Air. I heard *you* on Fresh Air. You're a famous author.

FANNY
Well, aren't you? If you're not you should relocate because this road is just for famous writers.

FRED
Well, I'm also an actor. Well. Wanted to be, but.

Fanny STOPS at a DRIVEWAY (or tree with POST NUMBER on it):

FANNY
Well. *My* knee hurts. So.

FRED
Right. Nice to meet you, Fanny. It's Fanny Wright, right?

FANNY
Right. And you're Fred.

FRED
Banks. Right. Well. Happy writing.

FANNY
Keep the dream alive, Fred.

She limps off.

7 EXT. FRED'S CABIN - NIGHT 7

THUNDER. The house looks small below an angry sky.

8 INT. FRED'S CABIN - NIGHT 8

INSERT: *RAIN* on the window. The storm begins...

Fred types something on his laptop:

INSERT: ***"Venus Fanny Right"***

SEARCH RESULTS: ***"Did you mean 'Fanny Wright'?"*** A handful of press about Fanny and her book; about how *VENUS* has been optioned as a film. *Vulture, NY Mag, The Atlantic,* etc.

Battery: 5%. We can just barely make out FRED'S DESKTOP BACKGROUND - his arm around a WOMAN, face obscured by SEARCH WINDOWS. He PLUGS in his charger.

He scrolls to the bottom, landing on an article from an obscure publication: ***"WHILE SCARY AS HELL, 'VENUS' MISSES THE MARK."***

FRED
You're not so great.

TOP SHOT (FROM THE LANDING) - The POWER GOES OUT. Fred is swallowed in DARKNESS, lit only by the SCREEN OF HIS LAPTOP.

FRED (CONT'D)
Nope.

LIGHTNING flashes.

INSERT - LIGHT SWITCH. We TILT UP as Fred approaches, flicking it *(nope)*. He towers over us, imposing.

FRED (CONT'D)
Got a flashlight around here, Mr. Torrance?

He searches some drawers. No dice.

He eyes THE CELLAR DOOR.

FRED (CONT'D)
(in a "Buffalo Bill" voice)
We got one in heeeere.

THUNDER. He chuckles to himself.

FRED (CONT'D)
You got a biiig imagination, Freddy.

His LAPTOP DIES, enveloping him in MORE DARK.

Another *FLASH OF LIGHTNING* ignites the WINDOW BEHIND HIM.

SOFT FOCUS: ***SOMEONE KNOCKS ON THE GLASS!***

Fred whips around, *SCREAMING!*

It's Fanny! Clutching an UMBRELLA and a FLASHLIGHT.

FANNY
(through the glass)
Is your power out!?

9 INT. FRED'S CABIN - NIGHT 9

LOW ANGLE INSERT - JUST AS with FRED EARLIER - Fanny drops a SOAKING WET DUCK UMBRELLA into frame.

She makes herself at home - kicks off rain boots, drops her soaked JACKET to the floor, then places her (still open) umbrella by the door.

FANNY
Just when I was really getting into the groove.

FRED
Sorry?

FANNY
I was writing. Power outage snapped me outta my- Know when you're writing and it feels like you're clutching the dorsal fin of a narwhal?

FRED
Do narwhal's have dorsal fins?

FANNY
No but you know how it's like, *HOLD ON, MAN!* And you know if you lose the narwhal, you may not see it again for 10 days? That was me. Minutes ago. Don't lose the narwhal. This place is small.

She puts her NOTEBOOK on the table.

FRED
All your million dollar ideas?

FANNY
Actually, yes.

FRED
What're you working on?

FANNY
Oh. I'm not gonna tell you.

FRED
Oh.

FANNY
Sorry if that's abrasive. But. Yeah, I don't "talk projects." People steal. Especially desperate white men like you.

FRED
Excuse me?

RACK FOCUS - Fanny turns from the hearth.

FANNY
Why don't you make a fire?

FRED
I, uh. I'd intended to.

10 INT. FRED'S CABIN - FIREPLACE ROOM - MOMENTS LATER 10

LIGHTNING brightens the driveway. It's coming down now.

FANNY
So, what are YOU working on?

FRED
Oh, I- a bunch of different things.

FANNY
A writing thing? You said you're a writer.

FRED
Oh, yeah. I'm doing this one about Korah? It's a religious epic.

FANNY
The rebel who went against Moses. Dope. Or is it the Korah of the Qur'an.

FRED
Uh. I'm still working that one out. I also have this one thing about a werewolf...

FANNY
Oof.

FRED
What?

FANNY
Werewolves.

FRED
Yeah. Scary.

FANNY
No. Trodden.

FRED
How is it trodden?

Fred's having a hard time starting a fire.

FANNY
Just let me do it.

She pushes him out of the way.

FANNY (CONT'D)
You need kindling.

FRED
Oh, yeah, no I know.

No, he doesn't. She starts making a fire.

FANNY
Werewolves are tough. There's American Werewolf in London and then there's everything else. Which is what. Silver Bullet?

FRED
Silver Bullet's good.

FANNY
Silver Bullet's campy, child garbage.

The wood IGNITES, warm and furious and crackling.

CLOSE on Fred, his face ORANGE WITH FIRE (and embarrassment).

FRED
Ouch.

REVERSE: Fanny stands into frame, HIGH FLAME behind her.

FANNY
Nice job, me! (beat) So. What's your werewolf tale?

She stokes the logs with the FIRE POKER.

FRED
Well. This. It's sort of a revenge story. Werewolf kills a guy's parents-

FANNY
A werewolf... kills a guy's parents.

FRED
Right, well, a little boy. He's a little boy at the time.

FANNY
At the time a werewolf kills his parents.

FRED
Tears 'em to pieces, yes. And he's like *"I'm gonna get revenge."* So it's sort of an action saga.

FANNY
That's a cool little boy voice. But, what's the story?

FRED
What do you mean? That's the story.

FANNY
No. That's the *idea.* What's it really about, man.

Ding. Fred's phone from beneath the cushions.

FRED
(reading the text)
Just because you're a bestselling author of one horror book doesn't mean you get to school me on story.

Did that hurt her?

FANNY
Well, geez Fred. Actually, yes. Yes it does.

Fanny takes a step toward Fred, who sits.

Flame shadows on their faces.

THUNDER, closer to the house than before.

Fanny suddenly looks... *imposing.*

FANNY (CONT'D)
Are you scared?

Fred eyes the FIRE POKER in her hand.

FRED
I don't love thunder. What. Nothing scares you?

FANNY
I love being scared.

She turns and pokes the fire.

Fred SLOWLY EMERGES from a WALL OF DARKNESS behind her.

SPOOKY MUSIC as Fred creeps toward Fanny...

HE ***ROAAARRSSSS*** AT THE TOP OF HIS LUNGS!

Fanny turns to Fred, unphased.

FANNY (CONT'D)
I have an idea.

FRED
Oh... kay.

FANNY
Do you have any alcohol?

An absolutely THRILLING ORCHESTRAL STING takes us to:

11 JUMP CUTS IN THE KITCHEN: 11

- A BEER is CRACKED OPEN.

- A 2nd BEER is CRACKED OPEN.

- VARIOUS INSERTS on FANNY'S HAND lighting FUNKY CANDLES.

12 INT. KITCHEN - NIGHT 12

We shoot the following in 50/50 PROFILES and 3/4 CLOSE-UPS:

FRED
Cheers.

FANNY
Cheers.

FRED
What's your idea?

FANNY
Scare me.

FRED
Sorry?

FANNY
You scare me, and I'll scare you.

FRED
What, like... What.

FANNY
Power's out. I'm bored. You're a scaredy cat.

FRED
Unfair.

FANNY
Let's tell each other scary stories.

FRED
I don't know any scary stories.

FANNY
Then we'll make 'em up! You're a writer.

FRED
You're the professional. I work in advertis-

FANNY
Shut the fuck up and use your imagination.

Fred blinks and drinks.

FANNY (CONT'D)
Come on, Fred. Story time. No judgies.

She grins, flames dancing in her pupils.

13 INT. FRED'S CABIN - FIREPLACE ROOM - MOMENTS LATER 13

WEIRD WIDE - Fred sits on the couch. He is not comfortable.

FANNY'S COVERAGE is CLOSER, warmer (*comfortable*).

FANNY
Okay. You first.

FRED
This was your idea.

FANNY
Tell me your werewolf story. *Chop chop, kiddies.*

FRED
Is that a Cryptkeeper impression? I love that show.

FANNY
Me too. Him and his puns. *Tonight's tale is about an axe murderer who loves to HALVE fun! HEhehehHEEH.*

Fred absorbs this for a long beat.

FRED
(halfway good impression)
Good evening, boys and GHOULS. May I AXE you a question?! HEeEEhehhhe.

FANNY
Werewolf. Go.

FRED
Okay, uh. So, starts with this little boy. And when he's asleep, a werewolf comes and kills his parents. (beat) And he witnesses it. It's traumatizing. He gets- he ends up getting adopted by this nice foster family. And they get dragged into this whole situation. They're in danger, like as older people, and so he has to track him down and get revenge before he gets to his loved ones.

FANNY
Jesus. Christ, dude.

FRED
Good story, right?

FANNY
Awful.

FRED
Huh. I thought you said "no judgies."

FANNY
We're literally fireside. Stand the fuck up and *TELL ME A STORY.* You're an actor, Fred.

FRED
Not, like. Professionally-

FANNY
Get up and CONJURE some fucking SCARES, dude. USE THE SPACE!

FRED
Who are you, Uta Hagen?

Fanny chugs beer.

FRED (CONT'D)
Fine. Fine.

He rubs his sweaty palms on his jeans.

FANNY
That's right. Warm up. *HE'S WARMING UP, EVERYBODY!* You know it's gonna be a good one!

FRED
Can you keep your voice down?

FANNY
What, are you afraid you're gonna wake the woman in the attic?

The EERIE NOTE of a VIOLIN.

She looks up and makes CREAKY FOOTSTEP SOUNDS out of the side of her mouth, tracking the eerie intruder with her eyes.

Fred reluctantly follows her gaze to the ceiling.

FANNY (CONT'D)
(Old Woman Voice)
LET ME OUTTTTTT!!!

FRED
JESUS, FANNY.

FANNY
LET'S GO, FRED! WE'RE BURNING MOONLIGHT. *SCARE ME MOTHERFUCKERRR!*

FRED
FINE! Shit!

14 INT. FRED'S CABIN - CONTINUOUS - "**WEREWOLF**" 14

Fred stands.

It takes a moment for Fred to warm up, but when he does, he *SHOWS* more than tells. And that's when it gets... ***fun.***

TRUCK-IN to FRED for the first time he's storytelling:

FRED
This little kid. It's his birthday. Let's call him... Sam. *Happy birthday dear Saaammm... Happy birthday to youuuuuu...*

He side steps, "acting" out the parents and Fanny **hums.**

FRED (CONT'D)
We see little Sam's parents. Clapping. Smiling. *Our little boy. I just can't wait to watch you grow up. What an incredible life we're going to give you.*

FANNY
That's a little on the nose isn't it? "*What an incredible life we're going to give you.*"

FRED
Hey. This is my story. I'm still working it out.

FANNY
Keep going.

Fred slams the rest of his beer.

FRED
That night, the boy - Sam - tosses and turns in bed. He looks out his bedroom window. A storm like this one. There's this scary, uh, *tree* making these creepy, crawly shadows like... like in Poltergeist.

He makes a stupid TREE-SHADOW PUPPET on the wall. He even makes *gnarled scraping-against-the-invisible-window* SOUNDS.

FRED (CONT'D)
But then. There's this... *noise*. And it's... downstairs. And Sam's mom and dad are in the room down the hallway - they hear it, too. Mom turns to dad: *There's someone downstairs*. So, dad heads down the stairs with a flashlight.

FANNY
Paint that picture, Fred. Gimme some fuckin' DETAILS.

FRED
His dad - whose name is Bill, also - uh, he has a mustache and a combover - he goes downstairs with- a flashlight! With one of those red flashlights you buy at a gas station!

FANNY
Fuck yes he does!

Fred grabs Fanny's FLASHLIGHT and shines it around the room.

FRED
Sam's dad, see, he's got a bad heart. He's breathing fast. But- he's the man of the house, what are you gonna do?

POV: FLASHLIGHT. We follow the light around the room, passing furniture, casting shadows, briefly blinding Fanny. (*"Hey!"*).

FRED (CONT'D)
He gets to the kitchen. And hears these... GRUNTS. Heavy, animal GRUNTS. And his hand shakes so the flashlight's shaking like...

FANNY
Show me the shaking, Fred!

His hand (and the light) TREMBLES.

FRED
OKAY I'm SHAKING! *H-honey!? Th- theres something in the k-kitchen!* He shines the light on the source of the noise. *What on earth is that blasted sound- GAH!*
It's... it's a... *RACCOON!* Y'know?

He makes some halfway decent RACCOON NOISES.

FRED (CONT'D)
And it's cute, kinda standing on its hind legs. A moment of quiet before...

Fred makes a pretty good GLASS SHATTERING NOISE.

HEAR - **SOUND DESIGN** - ACTUAL GLASS shatter.

Like I said - when these stories get good - when Fred and Fanny are on a ROLL - we start to HEAR things. Even **SEE things... their imagination blooms, and it gets **FUN*****

FANNY
GASP! What is it Fred?!

FRED
It's a GODDAMN WEREWOLF, FANNY!!!
This HULKING, HAIRY, INHUMAN...
(MORE)

FRED (CONT'D)
THING, TEN FEET TALL and uh like THREE FEET WIDE, SMASHES THROUGH THE WINDOW LIKE IT'S NOTHING.

FANNY
"Like it's nothing" love it.

Fred shoots her a look. *"Sorry."*

FRED
Dad screams. Shines the flashlight in the werewolf's face.

Fred spins, ducks, and pops back up as the werewolf, spotlighting himself with the flashlight. He ***ROARS!***

HEAR - FRED'S VOICE PITCH-SHIFT - LOW and TERRIFYING.

FANNY
That's good. That's the shit, Fred.

FRED
Yeah! The last thing Sam's dad sees before he dies is this hairy, fanged face. This werewolf that SLASHES THE SKIN CLEAN OFF HIS SKULL! *Agh my face a werewolf cut my face off!*

He mimics a screaming, dying dad - gargling blood. Fanny gives an enthused thumbs up ("enthused" for her, anyway).

Fred STANDS ON the CHAIR opposite FANNY, playing the MOM:

FRED (CONT'D)
Thanks. Standing at the top of the stairs is Sam's mom. *Oh my god, Oh my god. SAM GET IN THE CLOSET! NOW!*

Fred cups Fanny's face like mother to son. *"It's okay."*

FRED (CONT'D)
It's going to be okay.

FANNY
(smooshed cheeks)
Okay.

FRED
That's when they hear him. Lurking up the stairs. Lurking- what's the word, what's a better word-

FANNY
Lumbering.

FRED
Fucking LUMBERING up the stairs.

FANNY
Show me that lumber, Fred.

FRED
Yup.

Fred disappears into the darkness of the STAIRWELL. PAN along the wall as he lumbers up the stairs. ***THUMP. THUMP. THUMP...***

Fanny eats a fistful of CHIPS.

FANNY
Breathe like a werewolf.

HEAR: Fred *GRUNT* and *SNARL* through the cabin wall. It legit *SOUNDS* like a WEREWOLF. It's scary.

ZOOM to A WEREWOLF'S CLAWS wrapping around the frame of the UPSTAIRS DOORWAY. Fanny is entranced. *Now it's getting fun...*

FANNY (CONT'D)
That's good. That's scary, Fred.

Fred pokes around the corner. Totally normal.

FRED
See, I can be scary.

FANNY
Yup. Keep going.

FANNY'S POV: Fred continues his story from the 2nd level:

FRED
So this WEREWOLF lurks and lumbers and snarls up the stairs. And as he reaches the top steps, he sniffs the air, searching for his next victim.

Fred sniffs the air like a WEREWOLF, casting an epic, FIERY SHADOW on the wall.

FRED (CONT'D)
"I'm in here you son of a bitch!"

FANNY
She grabs a revolver out of the shoebox at the top of a closet.

FRED
How'd you? I mean-

FANNY
Obviously. It's just kind of an obvious... progression.

FRED
Why does it have to be obvious?

FANNY
They've done it in like 600 movies. Keep going.

Fred plays both mom - frantically loading the gun - and werewolf, hulking toward her.

FRED
Mom loads the gun, hands shaking. *"Shit shit shit!"* The werewolf is in the room now.

Fred takes the werewolf's place and snarls.

FRED (CONT'D)
THUMP. THUMP. THUMP.

He takes mom's place.

FRED (CONT'D)
Mom loads the last bullet. Closes the chamber. Cocks the hammer.

ANGLE ON: Fred's HAND, loading the last bullet, the unseen wolfman in the slanted hallway beyond.

HEAR - the satisfying *CLICK-CLICK* of gun metal.

FANNY
Are they silver bullets? She clearly knows what she's doing. Have they been through this before? She a cop?

FRED
Good point... Sam's in the closet trying life or death not to make a peep like-

FANNY
Laurie Strode in Halloween?

Fred nods, and huddles against the RAILING - playing young SAM now - shadows licking his face, covering his own whimpering mouth.

FRED
Sam watches the wolf... lumber... by the door toward his mom, trying SO hard not to make a peep. And that's when mom gets in firing position. *SMILE YOU SON OF A BITCH!*

FANNY (O.S.)
Very *Jaws*.

FRED
Favorite movie.

He mouths three *GUNSHOTS* - overlapped with the actual *CRACK* of gunfire - followed by the cacophony of a WAILING WEREWOLF.

We TRUCK-IN and DUTCH each time "Mom" fires.

FRED (CONT'D)
Did she kill him? NO! The wolf turns to mom and charges her. Mom screams as he BITES INTO HER JUGULAR! And Sam watches from the closet. HE CAN'T SCREAM!

He huddles again, holding his mouth with two trembling hands.

FRED (CONT'D)
SAAmMMmm, she utters with a bloody gargle. Her throat is all-

FANNY
Gurgle. A bloody *gurgle*.

FRED
RIGHT. She does a bloody GURGLE.

Fred impersonates a near-decapitated Mom, dropping the gun.

FRED (CONT'D)
So, she's dead. And now it's just Sam and the werewolf.

TENSE HORROR MUSIC as Fred's werewolf stalks for his young victim. We see the **werewolf hand** again at some point...

FRED (CONT'D)
And just as his clawed hand is about to open the closet door, SIREN LIGHTS THROUGH THE WINDOWS! *WHEEE-WEWW.* It's the COPS! The werewolf whips his head toward the commotion and he grunts, like, he's *PISSED.* And he jumps out the window!

A SIREN LIGHT GAG hits Fred's werewolf. He JOLTS, charging back down the stairs and across the room before HITTING HIS KNEE on the COFFEE TABLE.

FRED (CONT'D)
Fuck! Ow.

FANNY
Did the werewolf hit his knee in the coffee table or was that not intentional?

FRED
Funny.

FANNY
How'd the cops come?

FRED
They knew because-

He lifts the receiver off the cabin's ROTARY PHONE. It DROPS TO THE FLOOR with a ***thud.***

HEAR - faint DIAL TONE.

FRED (CONT'D)
She dialed 911 and left the phone on the ground.

He points to it, smug.

FANNY
So the werewolf gets away. The cops rescue young Sam... and then what?

Fred opens the FRIDGE and presses a FROZEN DINNER to his knee.

FRED
I haven't gotten that far, but I picture him growing up to be a bounty hunter-type who dedicates his life to finding his parent's killer. Good IP there. Video games, graphic novels...

FANNY
Plural! My immediate question is - obviously - DID the family know this werewolf. In real life. Was it the pervert neighbor? Bitten by some lycan? A *Lovely Bones* situation with a spooky twist?

FRED
I mean, that's good but, no. I dunno. I'm figuring it out.

FANNY
Uh huh. Does Sam get his revenge?

FRED
Yeah. Maybe he's been following this guy. Tracks him. Discovers his identity? Follows him to a diner with his mom's revolver he's been carrying for years.

FANNY
Finds out the guy's a creepy mechanic or something.

FRED
Sure. So his gun is loaded with silver bullets. He walks right up to him. In a diner or some shit.

WIDE PROFILE - Fred approaches Fanny like her nervous, would-be killer, keyed by firelight. As he looms over her:

FRED (CONT'D)
Excuse me, sir? Are you Ben... Franklin? I'm bad at coming up with names.

FANNY
No, I think it's interesting if a werewolf shared its name with the politician that discovered electricity.

FRED
Right. *Are you Ben Franklin?*

FANNY
Yeah. What's it to you?

FRED
Sam looks him in the eyes. He *knows.* He reaches for his gun. Everything goes into slow motion.

He does this. We WIDEN OUT to see the ridiculous image:

Fred pulling an invisible gun out from his waistband, making SLOW MOTION SOUNDS.

He points the gun to Fanny's head. And pulls the trigger.

FRED (CONT'D)
Splat.

A satisfied grin cuts across his face.

FRED (CONT'D)
End movie. Cue Huey Lewis. Credits.

15 INT. FRED'S CABIN - CONTINUOUS - "**GRANDPA**" 15

Fred plops down opposite Fanny and *HOWLS* like a werewolf.

FANNY
(unmoved)
Why not make Sam female?

FRED
Because I'm writing from personal experience.

FANNY
The... personal experience of a werewolf killing your parents? How'd you make it? You must HATE dogs.

FRED
(dropping the TV dinner)
Fanny.

FANNY
Too many white dudes in action movies. C'mon, John Wick. Pass the Bechdel Test. The best stories are mined from real life.

FRED
Well, I'm not a little girl in real life.

FANNY
It could be a saga if it was a bit more... if it had more substance.

FRED
If it had more, uh- okay.

FANNY
What's the *lineage*. Were Sam's parents the Matthew Rhys and Keri Russell of werewolf killing spies? Is little Sam the "Daywalker" of werewolves?

FRED
That could be good.

FANNY
I mean it's been done before, but.

FRED
Okay. It's a her. Sam's SAMANTHA now. 'Cuz I'm a RARE white guy. One that's actually inclusive of-

FANNY
All beings, gender confirming and non-conforming alike! Good!

FRED
And hand out a compliment, for Chrissake! I just made a fool of myself acting my heart out. Your turn, Strasberg.

FANNY
I'm good.

Fanny pokes at the fire. The room lights up.

FRED
The hell you mean you're *good*? You suggested we stay up and do scary story theatre. C'mon. Act out this "top secret" project.

FANNY
Oh, I couldn't possibly do that.

FRED
Why. You signed an NDA?

FANNY
Actually, yes.

FRED
Huh.

FANNY
All my stuff in development is top secret. So.

FRED
Well. Aren't you, uh. That's very cool. Well. You have to tell me *some* story. Tell me more about the woman in the attic.

FANNY
Hmm. Okay. I got one.

FRED
Shoot.

FANNY
It's based on a true story.

FRED
I'm hooked.

She sits in a rocking chair and keeps rocking.

FANNY
It's called *"GRANDPA."*

FRED
I'm freaked out already.

FANNY
And it's about a little girl who's haunted by her creepy, crawly grandpa.

FRED
If this is a kid-touchy story I don't wanna hear it, please.

FANNY
That's what makes it really scary. This girl, let's call her *Cassie*.
(MORE)

FANNY (CONT'D)
Every time Cassie was left alone with her grandpa by her mom - she was convinced he was gonna do *something*. There was something *off* about grandpa. Forget the fact he was Romanian or Russian and every time he spoke Cassie couldn't shake the thought he sounded like a damn vampire... It was the way grandpa's lazy eyes tracked Cassie turning on the TV to watch 'toons. How he'd sit, slumped at the end of the dining room table, which they hadn't had a real meal at since grandma died. His glorified coffee table, littered with stacks of old newspapers and nature magazines, conveniently dog-eared to pages with indigenous women baring their breasts. Smoking endless packs of Kent Kings. Imploring her to sit on his lap, to *"Come tell gvampa how is at school..."*

FRED
Okay, I'm good on this one.

FANNY
Shut up, I'm not going there. Cassie's mom was one of those hopeless Toni Collette characters that worked at a burger joint and smoked a pack a day. Before every shift, she'd bend down to Cassie's level, reeking of vulcanized eggs and drug store perfume. *Be nice to grandpa, sweetheart. He don't got long left.*

Fanny does a *great* smoker's voice.

FANNY (CONT'D)
Fucked up thing is she just left her alone at this house. Cassie would hide. Grandpa would look for her. Shuffling around in his pajamas, wheeling around his squeaky oxygen tank. Always knew when Grandpa was close 'cuz of that squeaky tank.

Fanny loosens an imaginary oxygen tank knob and makes the sound of AIR RELEASING with solid *rusted tank wheel* sounds.

FANNY (CONT'D)
"CASSSSSIEEEEE. CASSSSIEEE." Kinda fucked up how both our stories are about little girls running from monsters, huh? *"CASSSIEEE. I know you're in house. Hide and seek?"* And if grandpa wasn't bad enough, his mangy dog, Rover - matted, salt and pepper fur, and a shitty attitude. He'd snap at Cassie every time she'd get near him. And grandpa'd just shrug it off: *"Aw, Rover loves ya. More den gvampa, maybe! Nah. Just TEASINK'."* Grandpa was shit at conceiving names. You can imagine. *Rover.*

Fred rolls his eyes, drinks beer.

FANNY (CONT'D)
Cassie would sit up in her bedroom and barricade the door and scribble in her journal. Binding plastered with glitter n' kitty cat stickers. *How... To... Kill.. Gwandpaw...*

Fanny - as CASSIE now - scribbles in her NOTEBOOK and holds up a DOODLE of an OLD MAN WITH X's FOR EYES. She STANDS:

FANNY (CONT'D)
Cassie knew how much Grandpa liked his sloppy soups and room temp applesauce. So one day she decides to sneak into his medicine cabinet... and poison him. See what'd happen if she put more meds than usual in his food, anyway.

FRED
That's a fucked up kid...

FANNY
Come on, Fred. Kid logic. Like, *I'm being helpful! Maybe it'll kill him, maybe it won't. I'm 5!* She splits open his pill caps like a mini Paul Sheldon in Misery, emptying the contents into Gwandpa's soup. Sure enough, just as he's about to sip on the first gulp of toxic stew, gvampa's lil' ciggy cough quickly turns into a full blown emphysemic attack.

LOW ANGLE: Fanny keels over, COUGHING AT US.

FANNY (CONT'D)
A violent spasm sends the soup onto the floor. And, faster than he can say "down, boy!" Rover rushes over. And eats. *All of it.*

TRUCK IN to the invisible bowl on the FLOOR. We HEAR the *smacksmacksmack* of a DOG LAPPING UP SOUP. (Ew)

REVEAL: Fanny, standing in the corner, giving Fred side-eyes while making dog-lapping-up-soup sounds.

FRED
That makes me uncomfortable.

FANNY
Not long after Rover lap-lap-laps up the soup, grandpa's beloved ol' dog drops dead, right in front of 'em. Right there on the ciggy-burned-and-bourbon-stained carpet. As you can imagine, Grandpa was BESIDE himself.

Fanny drops to her knees and performs a shrill and dramatic and disturbing rendition of grandpa mourning his dead dog.

FANNY (CONT'D)
Grandpa's health declined. One night, grandpa's on his death bed in the house. Mom's in the kitchen doing dishes or something. *"Hey Cass, sweetheart? Can you feed grandpa his dinner? Thanks!" Oh, CHRIST*, she thinks. Cassie kneels bedside and shovels applesauce or greek yogurt or some shit into grandpa's sad, gross lil' mouth, but of course he's too devastated to eat and it's just spilling all over him like this...

Fanny spoons PEANUT BUTTER (or something Fanny is okay putting in her mouth) and obscenely SMEARS IT on her mouth.

FANNY (CONT'D)
"Caaaaassie. Come. I have secret for you. C'MERE." But, Cassie doesn't wanna *"c'mere."* But she does. Because she knows what she did. *Whatever. It'll be over soon.*
(MORE)

FANNY (CONT'D)
'Member what mama said: *"BE NICE TO GRANDPA. HE DON'T GOT LONG LEFT."*

Fred is wide-eyed. He no-look cracks open a FRESH BEER.

FANNY (CONT'D)
So, she leans in... *"You are happy, hm?" What? "I know you try poison my dinner, sveetheart."* And now his gnarly fuckin' smoker fingers are digging into Cassie's forearm. *"G-grandpa. You're hurting me." "Shhshhhh. I know you try to poison me. And I know you kill my doggy. And is so much worse."* Cassie's like, shaking. Beside herself. Her eyes brim with terrified tears.

Fanny - as Cassie - gets emotional.

FANNY (CONT'D)
"Th- that's n-not true, grandpa. That's not true at all. N-not t-" tears just *spilling* down her face. Grandpa pulls her in closer, tightening his skeletal grip around the flesh of his granddaughter's arm with the last of his strength... *"When I c-C-C-c-"* He starts choking, food all over his mouth-

Fanny gets food all over her mouth.

FANNY (CONT'D)
"I want you to know when I come back, I'm g-g- I am going to get you."

An ominous RUMBLE OF THUNDER. It's perfect timing.

FANNY (CONT'D)
Perfect timing.

FRED
Wow.

FANNY
Well. That gets Cassie crying.

Fanny bellows a series of slow, desperate (convincing) sobs. She pauses to splash beer on her eyelids for effect.

FANNY (CONT'D)
"Yes. Cry, sveetheart. Is so much worse.
(MORE)

FANNY (CONT'D)
You try to kill me but kill Rover instead. And is so much worse! AHHAHAHHahHAAHHAHAasdhaha!"

THUNDER. LIGHTNING. Fred is *legit* freaked. *Fanny's committed.*

FANNY (CONT'D)
Cassie's mom rushes into the room and kneels by her daughter who is INCONSOLABLE. Little does she know, it's not because she's sad. It's because she's *TERRIFIED.* Mom takes grandpa's hand in hers while Cassie subtly pries his other pale claw from her arm.

Fanny leans down next to Fred, taking his hand.

FANNY (CONT'D)
"Aw, papa. We're here. We're both here. Me n' Cassie. Cassie, your FAVORITE granddaughter. Well, only granddaughter. But favorite. She's your favorite." Stop saying favorite, mom. "Aw, sweetheart. I know ya loved your grandpa. Yes you did. It's alright." She wipes her daughter's tears and hugs her TIGHT, rocking her back and forth facing her dead grandpa whose dead mouth is open like this.

Fanny makes a twisted DEAD GRANDPA FACE.

FANNY (CONT'D)
Cassie's like *"Mom, um-" "Oh, shoot, sorry sweetheart!"* And she shield's Cassie's eyes from the dead body... facing her toward the wall, on which sits the one piece of art in the whole. Fucking. House. A portrait of Grandpa's beloved dog, Rover.

ANGLE ON: a legit PORTRAIT OF A DOG on the cabin wall.

FANNY (CONT'D)
Cue convenient moment of thunder and lightning...?

A convenient crash of THUNDER AND LIGHTNING.

FANNY (CONT'D)
Thank. You.

Fanny stands - woozy - hair falling over her face.

FANNY (CONT'D)
Couple years later, life returned to normal. Cassie was a student at Small Town Sugar Sweet Zero Evil High, or whatever. Mom started dating a nice man, one who wears a jean jacket lined with sheep fur and his name's "Chuck" probably.

FRED
What a detail.

FANNY
Quit her job at the diner. It wasn't long before Cassie felt comfortable being left alone. Mom and her fella let her stay at home on date nights. And one fall evening just days before Halloween, they leave Cassie alone to go to their favorite Italian place. Cassie pops some dumb movie in the VHS. Something innocuous.

FRED
Howard the Duck.

FANNY
Don't interrupt me?

FRED
Sorry.

Fanny sprawls out on the couch opposite Fred.

CLICK. A hint of an unseen TV GLOW edges Fanny's face.

FANNY
So, Cassie's all spread out on the couch, watching Howard the Duck. And the phone rings.

TILT DOWN to an INVISIBLE PHONE, now *RINGING.*

Fanny picks up. The moment the receiver comes off it's imaginary body - we HEAR *gross, heavy, WHEEZY BREATHING.*

(Fanny is the source, of course). Fred shifts in his seat.

FANNY (CONT'D)
"Hello?" "CAaaSsiieee." Oh no, she thinks. If it were a movie we'd dolly in reeeaaal slow...

We DOLLY-IN (reeeaaal slow) as Fanny continues...

FANNY (CONT'D)
"Cassssiieeee. Do you know who dis is? It's G-gGAGg-"

She lets out a vile, CORPSE-Y COUGH.

FANNY (CONT'D)
"It's graaaandpaaaa." Cassie's face is just dead white. She's *sick* with fear. *"I told you I was gonink to get you."* And that's when she hears footsteps in the *HOUSE, Fred. THUMP. SHUFFLE. SHUFFLE. THUMP.*

Fred swallows hard.

FRED
Nice sound effects.

FANNY
Don't interrupt me. So Cassie's thinking, *well what do I do. Grab a knife?*

Fanny pulls an imaginary knife out of nowhere.

HEAR: the **SCHINK** of the knife unsheathed to action.

FANNY (CONT'D)
She approaches the staircase. *Whatever's in the house... it's close.* She sees him.

CLOSE: Fred looks around, *freaked*.

FOLLOW FANNY to the stairwell - she stops in a PROFILE.

REVERSE: We TRACK the INVISIBLE DOG down the stairs.

FANNY (CONT'D)
Standing at the top of the stairs is a big. Black. Mangy. Dog. Cassie calls his name with a squeak: *"R-R-Rover?"* The dog traipses down the stairs with a sickly gait, one cockeyed leg in front of the other.
(MORE)

FANNY (CONT'D)
And prowls right toward Cassie, real slow. Gets right up to her face. Nose to nose.

Fanny gets on her hands and knees and *CRAWLS TO FRED*, head low like a predator.

Fanny gets NOSE TO NOSE with Fred, who pushes himself all the way back on the couch.

Fanny emits a long, ominous *GROWL*. We PITCH SHIFT the growl - which begins "human" and grows *supernatural.*

VFX: For a split second, her EYES have a REFLECTIVE GLINT.

FANNY (CONT'D)
The door OPENS BY ITSELF.

SOFT FOCUS in BACKGROUND: ***THE FRONT DOOR OPENS BY ITSELF!***

POV: DOOR - Fanny approaches the frame, unfazed.

FANNY (CONT'D)
And just as this ghostly dog slips into the night, Cassie's mom saunters in chuckling with Chuck, to find her daughter, pale as a toilet, clutching a knife. *"Sweetheart?"* Cassie turns to mom and points the knife in her face.

Fanny SWINGS AROUND, driving the unseen KNIFE toward us.

FANNY (CONT'D)
DON'T. CALL ME THAT.

ANGLE ON: Fred, captivated on the couch. *"Whoa."*

16 INT. CABIN - NIGHT (CONTINUOUS) 16

FANNY
Well I need a break. Let's order a pizza.

She snatches Fred's phone.

FANNY (CONT'D)
What do you want?

FRED
Anything but Hawaiian.

FANNY
How white of you.

FRED
What's with this "white guy" shit? You're white. Are you one of these "white men are the death of society" feminist... people?

She dials.

FANNY
I'm ordering YOU a pizza, aren't I? Hello? Hi. Can I order a half cheese half... veggie? The address is uh-

Fred jumps, grabs the "Welcome Sheet". He can't find it. Fanny snatches the paper and finds it instantly.

FANNY (CONT'D)
88 Bonnie Mountain Lane. (beat) An hour? (sticks her tongue out) They're a little backed up. Been some power outages. (to phone) WHATEVER! YES! PIZZA GOOD! See ya.

She hangs up. Fred reaches for his phone. Fanny retracts.

FANNY (CONT'D)
Oh my! Meredith's texting you. *"You're a monster."* Who's Meredith?

FRED
Oh, shit. Gimme that.

FANNY
Who is she?

FRED
My ex.

FANNY
Ex. What'd you do, you monster?

FRED
Give me my phone.

FANNY
C'mon, humor m-

FRED
I SAID GIVE ME MY FUCKING PHONE. OR YOU CAN GO BACK TO YOUR BIGGER, BETTER FUCKING CABIN.

A quick beat.

FANNY
I'm gonna take a walk.

She tosses Fred his phone.

FRED
Thanks. Sorry. A little privacy'd be great.

17 EXT. CABIN - NIGHT 17

Fanny rounds the PATIO, exhaling vapor.

THROUGH THE WINDOW: Fred paces. The RAIN drowns out what looks and sounds like a stressful conversation.

LIGHTNING emblazes the porch.

Fanny hits her CBD PEN and scribbles in her NOTEBOOK.

SOFT FOCUS through the window - we notice Fred staring at Fanny as he speaks into the phone. Fanny turns back toward the house just as Fred turns, continues pacing.

THUNDER sends her gaze forward, staring into the stormy dark.

More LIGHTNING - ILLUMINATING THE WOODS.

TRUCK-IN toward the woods. Lightning in the sky.

Is SOMETHING OUT THERE?

Fanny shrugs, unsatisfied by the answer.

We slowly TRUCK BACK, revealing A SHAPE IN THE FOREGROUND.

MAN'S VOICE (O.S.)
I'M DONE.

Fanny JUMPS. It's Fred.

FANNY
JESUS DICKS. Hi.

FRED
What's that?

FANNY
CBD. I should've given you some. Maybe you wouldn't have freaked the fuck out.

FRED
Should've given me some before my ex told me about the "protection notice" she's filing against me.

FANNY
Protection notice. You mean a restraining order.

Fred looks at her for a tense beat.

FRED
It's not what you think. May I?

Fanny offers her PEN. TWO SHOT / RAKE FRED & FANNY:

FRED (CONT'D)
I took her for granted. All a sudden, she wants to end it. Big surprise. Kicks me out. Big surprise. Find out there may have been *another guy. BIG* surprise. I write her some letters. Call her one or two hundred times. And threatened to kill her.

Fanny turns to Fred.

FRED (CONT'D)
I'm kidding. Kind of. We threatened to kill *each other*, honestly. You know when you're arguing with your, uh- I don't know if you have uh- But you're like, *"I'm gonna fucking kill you."*

FANNY
You're not putting me at ease.

FRED
I shouldn't have said anything. Anyway, I got a shrink. I might hate my life, but I got my shit together.

FANNY
Why do you hate it?

FRED
Well. Look at you. You're, what-

FANNY
A woman.

FRED
No. How *old* are you?

FANNY
Don't ask me how hold I-

FRED
I'm 38. You're living your dream. And your dream isn't rocket science. No offense.

FANNY
Well. Gee, Fred. Thanks.

FRED
Sorry.

FANNY
Instead of being like literally everyone else - *talking and not doing* - make a move, dude. Quit your job and outdo me.

FRED
Sounds easy enough. I'm on it.

FANNY
Now let's get inside. You owe me a story.

Fanny leaves Fred for a moment. He stares into the rain.

SPOOKY MUSIC SWELLS.

CUT TO:

18 INT. FRED'S CABIN - FIREPLACE ROOM - NIGHT - **"TROLL"** 18

FAST CLOSE-UPs with <u>limited</u> overlap:

FANNY
Hit me, Scaremaster.

FRED
Why don't you tell me about Venus?

FANNY
Why?

FRED
Because it's a classic. For those of us who don't know what Venus is.

FANNY
"Those of us." This isn't a movie. We don't need to establish shit.

FRED
Establish with me. I haven't read it.

FANNY
I thought you said you were a fan.

FRED
Maybe!

FANNY
You haven't read my book but you happen to know I'm the author.

FRED
Only because you told me who you are. I don't read a lot.

FANNY
Reading and writing makes a good writer. That's a Stephen King quote. Not verbatim, but.

FRED
Well, I'm pretty sure I can just write and watch movies and be good at it.

FANNY
I'm confident that's the quickest way to be a regurgitative hack.

TILT DOWN - she jots something down in her notebook.

FRED
What are you writing?

FANNY
Ideas. Real writers? We jot ideas.

FRED
Your golden ideas.

FANNY
Something like that.

FRED
Venus. Go.

FANNY
No.

FRED
Humor me.

FANNY
It's your turn.

FRED
It's gonna take me a minute to think of one.

FANNY
Blew your load with "Boy Who Cried Werewolf"?

Fred CATAPULTS out of his chair and paces around the room.

He begins stretching his legs and gets into a LOW SQUAT.

FANNY (CONT'D)
If this next story is about an evil man who shits out a more evil poop, I commend you.

FRED
That's a good one but no. I used to do this thing to scare my little brother when we were kids. I'd get real low and talk like this.

Fred walks with an unsettling waddle and speaks with a strained, freakish chortle:

FRED (CONT'D)
I'm a sCARy TRoOOOLLL.

FANNY
That's scary.

FRED
DoOO I FREAek You OuT.

FANNY
That's actually scary, Fred. Good start.

FRED
I'm a creepy little TROLL MAN.

FANNY
You sound a lot like Gollum from Lord of the Rings. What's your story, little troll? Do you live under a bridge?

Fred changes voices.

FRED
I DO. I do live under a bridge.

FANNY
It'd be better if he lived someplace weird. The air ducts of an office. An edible arrangements company.

HEAR: an *OFFICE PHONE RING.* Fanny "picks up":

FANNY (CONT'D)
Hi, Baskets You Can Eat? Sorry one moment, there's a troll in the wall?

FRED
Oh that's good. New guy at work, er, new *GIRL*, sorry. Karen. That's a good name for an unsuspecting new hire, yeah?

FANNY
Why not.

FRED
Karen interviews for a job. Old boss is all *Here at "Baskets You Can Eat" sure the name SOUNDS cute and sure we're a bunch of sweet, simple folks working in this small coastal town in Maine where nothing bad happens 'cept! We got one small secret: There's an evil troll in our ceiling!*

Fred chuckles. He's having fun.

FANNY
"Oh, him? Nothing to be afraid of. Nothin' at all. If you don't fuck with the troll, the troll won't fuck with you.
(MORE)

FANNY (CONT'D)
Have a nice day!" They wouldn't curse. They'd be more like *"Mind your baskets, and the troll will mind his."* I like that that's something people say at an edible arrangements company. *"Mind your baskets."*

FRED
A bunch of people's lunches go missing. *"Hey, has anyone seen the PB&J my wife made for me? **WAS IT THAT TROLL?!"*** The whole office turns in sync. Do it with me.

FANNY ENTERS FRAME. They EMBODY A CROWD OF CO-WORKERS and bring their FINGERS TO THEIR LIPS: ***"Shhh."***

FANNY
Love it.

FRED (CONT'D)
Oh, wow yeah. That is freaky.

<u>LIGHTING CHANGE</u> - It suddenly feels "**after hours**."

FANNY
That night, Karen's all alone, crunching the numbers of all the baskets that are edible, of course, and she hears a *VOICE*. *"Is... s-s-s-s-someone th-there?"*

Fred JUMPS to action, searching the room.

FRED
GASP! He's in the vents!

He tosses a piece of KINDLING across the room.

THUNK. As if cued, the room is suddenly a SOUNDSCAPE of HURRIED FOOTSTEPS UP THE WALL and ACROSS THE CEILING.

We WHIP FRANTICALLY to catch a glimpse of the creature.

FRED (CONT'D)
RUMBLE. CRUNCH. BANG. TAPTAPTAP. Things moving around the room.

FANNY
Like in Labyrinth when you can see the trolls skitter around her room!

FRED
Yeah, yeah! She hears this banging and fumbling around. And then:

THUNK. The room falls silent. No rain, even.

FRED (CONT'D)
THERE!

Fred HURDLES OVER THE COUCH and SHAKES IT, making "strained grunts": *EHEH EHEH.. MEH.. MEH...*

Fred reveals himself as "DEVIN THE TROLL"

FRED (CONT'D)
HELLOOooOOO KAaAaREnnn!

Fanny digs it, playing right along.

We FOLLOW BEHIND FRED - TROLL LEVEL - approaching Fanny.

FANNY
H-h-hi.

FRED
Hiiiiii.

FANNY
How do you know my n-n-name?

FRED
I'm a TROOLLL that's WHY. Hey. Happy birthday.

FANNY
Th-thanks so much. Wh-what's your name?

FRED
I'm... D- Devin. Devin the Troll.

FANNY
Devin, huh? You sound a lot like Smigel, Devin.

FRED
(changing voices)
Mhmm. Yup. I've come to grant you a birthday wish. What do you want. Anything in the world.

FANNY
I... I wish I could say goodbye to my dad. I never got to say goodbye.

A legit TEAR rolls down Fanny's cheek. She is IN character.

Fred lets out a MANIACAL TROLL CACKLE.

FANNY (CONT'D)
What the hell are you laughing at?

FRED
Woman! I can't grant you a WISH!

FANNY
Wh-what? Why not?

FRED
Because I'm... Just a troll that lives in a ceiling, is that enough of a reason for ya?

FANNY
Why are you *here,* troll?

FRED
I don't... know. Story wise.

FANNY
C'mon, Fred. Stop thinking. Is it a curse?

FRED
Uh- yeah, or-

FANNY
Maybe because, deep down, you're a GOOD troll... *drawn to the INTENTION of this place 'cuz the owner - who since died - was pure of heart and he set out to, with the gift of making arrangements-*

FRED
That are edible-

FANNY
-correct - *make people HAPPY.* But his evil dickhead misogynist son turned the mission around. And the troll got stuck here or something.

FRED
Or, I'm just an old troll who woke up from a long slumber and I'm hungry for the taste of human flesh. My leg's falling asleep sorry.

Fred kicks his leg out.

FRED (CONT'D)
SAY. Karen. Do you like making people happy?

FANNY
Yes. Yes I sure do like making people happy, Devin the Troll.

Fred's troll leans into a GRUESOME, SHADOWY CLOSE-UP.

FRED
Me too. (beat) Kill your boss.

FANNY
M-my boss? B-b-but... why?

FRED
Because he's a bad, bad man. He's a real creep to the girls around here and I want you to stick him like a pig. Kill him, and you'll turn this place around! And if you don't... I'll kill you and everyone you know. Heh!

FANNY
Oh. Okay...

FRED
Tomorrow night. He'll be working late. Do it then. And I'll be. RIGHT. THERE. WATCHING.

FANNY
Th-that's a tall order to ask someone to kill... someoene. Wh-what's in it for me?

FRED
I- *I don't know... story wise-*

FANNY
What if not only does she have to kill the boss, but kiss the troll to seal the deal. Then she gets to live for 300 years or something.

FRED
Oh, yeah. That's good. *Kill your boss and then kiss me. If you do, you'll live 300 years.*

FANNY
You're too ugly to kiss.

FRED
You literally just told me to say that.

FANNY
You make a fair point, Devin the Troll. Kill a shitty man, make the world a better place, live to see my grandchildren's children's children and kiss a troll, also? Seems like a lot of rules, but you got yourself a DEAL!

They shake on it. Fred lets out his best gleeful cackle and breaks character, nursing his sleeping legs. He rests against the wall.

FRED
Karen goes about her business. Sells some edible baskets. And the day comes where she's working late, as is her seemingly harmless boss. She ducks into his office, heart POUNDING. And he's NOT THERE. *Looking for something?*

FANNY
Some-someone, actually. I was looking for you. And suddenly all her doubts about this dude are out the window. As sure as he is a creep, he moves on Karen...

Fred watches Fanny back herself into a corner and sexually harass... herself. It's uncomfortable.

PROFILE ON FANNY - FIRE in the background. Fred SOFT FOCUS.

FANNY (CONT'D)
...pressing himself against her. Rubbing his creepy boner through his K-Mart khakis. Breath like an old peanut butter and jelly and sour milk sammich.

FRED
Ew.

FANNY
Hey! You gotta EMPATHIZE with our girl! Make us *WANNA KILL* this motherfucker. So, Karen's backed into a corner, surrounded by treat-filled baskets.
(MORE)

FANNY (CONT'D)
Which is *IRONIC* given the context. All the bright, colorful confections. Sugar-glazed bullshit to help people forget their lives.

FRED
So Karen's cornered. And she's thinking, *How am I gonna kill this creep.* Sure enough, on the table-

FANNY
SCISSORS.

She makes "invisible SCISSORS" with her hand.

HEAR: a metallic *"SNIP-SNIP"* outta thin air.

PROFILE - Fred & Fanny face one another, KITCHEN BEHIND THEM.

FRED
But he's got her by the shoulders. He's complimenting her on how great she smells. Which is <u>also</u> ironic 'cuz he smells like a peanut butter-

FANNY
Dirty diaper.

FRED
An ADULT diaper. Full of sour cream.

FANNY
OH-kay.

FRED
But whatever! He's disgusting! And she's eyeing the scissors and this guy's hands are starting to wander. *"I can't go through with this."*

FANNY
Yes. *I've never KILLED anyone before,* Karen thinks to herself.

FRED
How much does LIVING another 300 years really MEAN to me?

FANNY
And she's looking off in the corner - two lil' beady yellow eyes in the darkness of the air duct.

SLOW ZOOM to TWO BEADY EYES in the darkness of the kitchen.

FANNY (CONT'D)
That's the dishwasher... Right?

FRED
Isn't the power out.

SPECIAL - POV EYES FROM KITCHEN (time permitting).

FANNY
Stay in it.

FRED
'Kay. *"COME ONNNNN... Don't be a COWARDDDD. COME ONNNNN!"*

FANNY
He must really want that kiss.

Fred shrugs as the troll, low to the ground.

FANNY (CONT'D)
And that's when her pig boss says something that makes her snap. Something condescending. Like *You're such a good girl.* Or-

FRED
You've got a LOT to learn, kid. I make a great teacher...

FANNY
Too on the nose. Think shitty, but subtle. *"You bore me,"* but - again - the guy's fully erect.

FRED
DO IT! IF YOU DON'T DO IT I'LL DO IT MY DAMN SELF!

FANNY
Karen SNAPS.

Fanny *"Fight Clubs"* herself, kicking him/herself in the balls, clawing at him/herself, then BREAKS FREE!

FANNY (CONT'D)
She rushes to his desk. (*"Karen! Wait!")* Grabs the scissors and *STABS HIM RIGHT IN THE THROAT!*

Fanny does a convincing *just-been-stabbed-in-the-throat-by-a-pair-of-scissors* death dance.

FRED
UH oHhHHHH. The troll points to the door behind her, giggling.

FANNY
OH, YEAH. Standing there clutching a stack of papers, is the guy's mousy secretary. Who just ran back in to get something.

Fred RUSHES INTO FRAME BEHIND HER, now "MOUSY SECRETARY."

FRED
"Karen?!"

FANNY
"Barbara?! Um. It's, uh. It's not what it, uh... Looks like?"

FRED
And that's when the troll's like *"KILL HER TOO!"* But Barb makes a run for it!

FANNY
ACTION MUSIC! DRUMS! Dumdumdummmm!

And WE HEAR ACTION MUSIC! Pretty much in Fanny's rhythm.

FANNY (CONT'D)
And a chorus of screams. *OOO-AHHH! OOOO-AH!* Gothic. A gothic, scary ghoul choir.

HEAR: the sting of a *SCARY, GOTHIC CHOIR!*

Fanny assumes the role of the SECRETARY and SHRIEKS! She RUNS into the darkened living room and Fred follows suit.

<u>WE COVER THE FOLLOWING IN WIDE SHOT (that'll soon TRUCK-IN)</u>:

Fanny PRATFALLS INTO THE DARK OF THE KITCHEN - covering half We just see her legs. <u>Fred follows suit as the TROLL</u> and "DRAGS" her the dark.

FANNY (CONT'D)
Noo! He's eating me alive! I'm being eaten by a TROLL!!! HELP!!!!

She switches positions exposing her UPPER TORSO now.

Fred DRAGS her back into the kitchen. Fanny LAUGHS O.S.. They're having fun... HOLD on the EMPTY FRAME, as Fred and Fanny's laughter dies; as they compose themselves.

CAMERA now TRUCKS-IN as they crawl into view, sitting shoulder-to-shoulder in the frame of the kitchen.

FANNY (CONT'D)
And now with both deeds done, the troll approaches the woman. (Do it?)

FRED
(Oh, yeah). *"You did GOOD. Great teamwork back there."*

FANNY
He'd probably be more official, like, *"A murderous streak I'll dredge of you yet, m'lady. How about that KISS?"*

FRED
And the troll leans in.

FANNY
And so does she.

FRED
Three hundred years of life...

FANNY
Doesn't sound so bad.

Their lips are NEAR TOUCHING.

A FIGURE EMERGES FROM THE DARK BETWEEN THEM:

MAN'S (O.S.)
EXCUSE ME.

FANNY
WHOAA!

FRED
WHAAA!

Fred and Fanny EXPLODE to their feet, Fanny immediately pointing the fire poker ahead.

Fred scrambles for the flashlight and shines it on:

CARLO
WHOA! SORRY! I'm Carlo!

FRED
Uh huh?!

FANNY
And who the fuck are you, Carlo!?

CARLO (an Upstate NY pizza delivery guy) stands in the living room holding a LARGE PIZZA in a foam CARRYING CASE.

CARLO
Pizza! I'm the pizza guy! Sorry! Don't fuckin-! Sorry! Sorry to scare you!

Fanny and Fred stare for an embarrassed beat.

FANNY
Oh, it's fine.

FRED
You didn't scare us.

CARLO
Oh yeah no I scared you because ya'll just screamed, but um. Large half cheese, half veggie, am I wrong?

FANNY
Yes, why thank you, Carlo. I'm starving. It's Fred's treat.

Fred hands Carlo CASH.

CARLO
Wow. Nice tip!

FRED
My pleasure.

CARLO
Well. Enjoy your evening. I'm just glad you weren't all killing each other. Perfect night to do it!

He makes a pretend STAB motion, which <u>turns into acting out an elaborate MURDER</u> voicing victims, stabs and all.

CARLO (CONT'D)
Just kidding, that was creepy. Kidding.

FRED
Have a goodnight.

He goes to shut the door. Fanny GRABS it.

FANNY
Wait!

CARLO
OH! Right! Paper plates! They're in my car. I'll run n' get 'em.

FANNY
You strike me as fella who likes scary stories.

Fred slowly turns to Fanny.

19 INT. FRED'S CABIN - KITCHEN TABLE - NIGHT 19

Fred, Franny, and now CARLO sit at the CANDLELIT table, chowing on slices. Carlo nods at the TOWER of PAPER PLATES.

CARLO
You'd think I'd get tired of our pizza, but. No. Best in town. Best in the area, to be honest.

He takes another slice with the first slice in his mouth.

FRED
So, Carlo. What kinda name's Carlo?

CARLO
Oh, it's, um-

He says something incoherent, spitting pizza on himself.

CARLO (CONT'D)
Sorry, pizza mouth over here. *CARLO*. It means- I'm not sure what it means, but my mom and dad loved cars and I think it's some take on "Carl" also?

He takes a bite.

FANNY
Right on, so my friend Fred and I, we're riding out the storm telling each other scary stories.

CARLO
That sounds cool. So you guys are like, what, a coupla boy scout leaders?

A very, VERY long beat.

FANNY
No.

FRED
We're writers. Well. Fanny is. I'm not famous.

CARLO
Haha. Ouch. Emancipated much? Hahah! Wait. No. What's the word? Emancipated. No. EMASCULATED! Emasculated!

Fred shrugs, stung.

CARLO (CONT'D)
Kidding! Haha kidding, pal. Chin up. Jeez.

FRED
Have you heard of Venus?

FANNY
Let's not.

CARLO
The book? Of course.

FANNY
Let's not, Fred.

Fred just points to Fanny.

FRED
That's her. Big time.

CARLO
Wait. WOW. You wrote *Venus?*

FANNY
Uh huh.

CARLO
You wrote Venus?

FANNY
Uh huh.

CARLO
You wrote VENUS? Okay. *THAT'S* awesome.

FRED
Yeah you came just in time, too, Carlo, cuz it's Fanny's turn to tell a story.
(MORE)

FRED (CONT'D)
She's a great storyteller and you're in for a treat, so buckle up, you're welcome. Welcome.

CARLO
Wow. Okay. What'd I miss?

FANNY
A kid gets revenge on a werewolf, a fucked up grandpa and his ghost dog, and a troll that haunts an edible arrangements place. So far.

CARLO
Damn.

FRED
What's it gonna be, Fanny?

FANNY
Carlo's our guest. Carlo should get to pick who tells the story and what it's about.

CARLO
Wowww, thank you. That is a honor. Um. Dope. Do one about dead babies!

Fred and Fanny just look at Carlo.

CARLO (CONT'D)
I dunno. Just. Spitballin'.

He drinks SODA.

CARLO (CONT'D)
An army of dead babies? *Undead Babies with Rully Bad Scabiesssss* I dunno. I'm not a writer, or whatever. You're the writers, but.

FRED
How about a kid with a weird illness? He's turning into, like, a ghoul in school. There's a title. "A Ghoul in School."

CARLO
Too Ghoul for School!

FANNY
THAT'S hilarious, Carlo! I'm gonna write that down.

Fanny scribbles this in her notebook. COVERAGE CHANGES.

FRED
You can't write that down.

FANNY
Why not?

FRED
That's not your idea.

FANNY
It's not anyone's *idea*, Fred. It's a title. I'm writing a *title*.

CARLO
Yeah, I thought of it and I don't even care.

FRED
Can you stay out of this, please?

CARLO
Ouch. Okay, but. Ouch.

FANNY
Boys. BOYS. Relax.

They look at her.

FANNY (CONT'D)
Now who'd like to do some cocaine?

They slowly turn to Fanny.

POV: FANNY. Carlo slowly raises his hand.

20 INT. FRED'S CABIN - FIREPLACE ROOM - MOMENTS LATER 20

TOP SHOT - Fanny lays out a few lines of coke on the table.

FANNY
Sorry, I don't have a lot.

FRED
Writing retreat without "enough" drugs. How do you survive?

FANNY
I don't see you offering anything.

FRED
You're drinking my booze aren't you?

Fanny drinks BEER, shrugs.

FRED (CONT'D)
Huh. Well, I don't do drugs.

CARLO
Never done coke, dude?

FANNY
You've never done coke?

Fred quietly slides a slice of pizza onto his plate.

FANNY (CONT'D)
YOU'VE NEVER DONE *COKE*, you pussy!?

FRED
I'm not a pussy I'm just- I have too much energy to do coke. You wouldn't want to see me on coke. If I did it.

SECONDS LATER

Fred does a LINE OF COKE.

Fanny observes, smiling. She too does a LINE.

CARLO
Lemme do one more?

Carlo nudges in, does a LINE.

CARLO (CONT'D)
That's really good, uh, Fur- Fern-?

FANNY
Fanny. Yup. Thanks.

CARLO
DUH. Here I am goin', "Fu-Fuhhh... *Elmer Fudd?!"* No. Too good looking.

Carlo does ANOTHER. He sops up what he can with his fingers.

FANNY
Hey, slow down Sean Penn.

CARLO
Haven't done that shit since I was in college.

FRED
Where'd you go to college?

CARLO
Community.

FRED
Gotcha.

FANNY
Okay. Scare time, people.

CARLO
Fu-Fu-Fu-Fanny Fanny Bo-Banny Can't waaaaaait!

FRED
Why don't you do *VENUS*?

FANNY
C'mon Fred. This is an evening of original work.

FRED
It's a special occasion, Fanny. You've got a big fan present! He'd love to see you perform your life's work ow my nose.

CARLO
Not my words but not wrong, either!

FRED
And I haven't read it. Enlighten me! I bought dinner, didn't I?

FANNY
You buy me dinner and you expect a story?

FRED
Yeah. Yeah I do.

INSERT - a CORKSCREW ***STABS*** INTO CORK.

INSERT - Fanny uncorks a BOTTLE OF WINE - *"POP."*

21 INT. CABIN - CONTINUOUS - "**VENUS**" 21

She STANDS INTO a NEW FRAME, drinks:

FANNY
Venus.

CARLO
By Fanny Wright! WHOO! Sorry, I just kicked this uh- I don't know what this thing is, sorry.

Carlo picks up whatever CABIN RELIC he kicked over.

Fanny and Carlo proceed to perform a VERY FAST, *VERY* COKED UP TWO-HANDER of Fanny's best-selling book, *VENUS*.

It's frantic and messy and giggly and Fred is overwhelmed.

FANNY
Venus is the story of a young mother and son who go to the Catskills for 4th of July weekend. But before we get to them and their hot car ride up 278, toward the cool and dreamy countryside, we first meet Buddy.

CARLO
WHO IS A BADASS AND THE MAIN CHARACTER, PRETTY MUCH! He's the main character. WELL SORRY, *ONE* OF THE MAIN CHARACTERS. SORRY. Don't wanna take away from the others.

FANNY
Thanks, Carlo! Buddy *is* a badass! We come upon this man-

CARLO
Buddy!

FANNY
Yes! Buddy - sitting cliffside, overlooking the Catskills. He looks down at his hands.

CARLO
He's got these like, scars. And it's like, *FROM WHAT?!* Later we find out-

FANNY
Spoiler alert! So Buddy's in the woods and he hears something!

CARLO
IS HE HEARING THINGS?! Or is it *something else?!*

FANNY
Thanks, Carlo! Soon to find out.

CARLO
And when we do it's like.

Carlo does a weird "mind blown" gesture.

FANNY
Fred you look like you'd rather be anywhere else?

FRED
No I don't.

Fanny moseys around the room. She doesn't act this one out so much as <u>*CATAPULT*</u> through it. For obvious reasons.

(Coke)

FANNY
Bah-bah-bah-bahhh Buddy! encounters an abandoned cabin in the woods.

CARLO
It's a lot like your place, Fred!

FRED
It's not my place.

FANNY
It's not his place.

FANNY (CONT'D)
He goes inside. Place is a mess. Overturned furniture. Broken glass.

CARLO
Rotten food. It's like, *the fuck happened here,* y'know? Fred? Right?

FRED
Uh huh.

CARLO
HE HEARS SOMETHING IN THE NEXT ROOM!

FRED
Jesus. Shouting.

He walks delicately - like a DEER - behind Fanny.

CARLO
It's a DEER. That. Part. Scared. The living. SHIT. Outta me!

FANNY
I DID MY JOB! Buddy notices a picture of a cute little girl on the mantle.

CARLO
Buddy DOES NOT feel good about this place. He's like, *AH! NO!*

Fred smiles, like *"I get it."*

Fanny starts doing a weird "distant little girl cry".

FANNY
Buddy's thinking... That... is that a child?

CARLO
A LITTLE FUCKING GIRL! JUST LIKE FROM THE PHOTO. So scary, Fred.

FRED
So many stories about girls in distress tonight, huh?

FANNY
Fred.

CARLO
I wasn't here? But-

Fred brings a finger to his lips, shushing himself.

ON FANNY, then WIDEN to REVEAL CARLO:

FANNY
Buddy steps outside and just feet from the house is this *LITTLE GIRL*. She's crying against this tree.

CARLO
And Buddy's thinking, *well SHIT, someone killed her fuckin' parents! Or some THING, y'know!?* Scary.

FANNY
Buddy approaches the girl. She's little, poor thing. Her pink lil' Oshkosh's *are stained with blood.*

CARLO
And she's not crying a normal ordinary cry like "WAHah" she's crying a weird, sick fuckin' gargoyle vomit child cry like-

Carlo does a "GARGOYLE VOMIT" CRY against an imaginary tree.

FANNY
Meanwhile, mom and her young son, remember them? In the hot car?

CARLO
I sure do. *Beep beep!*

FANNY
They make a pit stop along the way. In the mid-80s, did I say that? It's in the mid-80s. And at a rest stop, the kid steps into a gift shop, Reagan's on TV and the kid's mom buys him a cap gun. And again it's the 80s, no cell phones which is a BIG deal-

CARLO
(take forever to yell it)
It's a BIG DEAL FRED BECAUSE SHIT. IS GONNA HIT. THE FAN!

FANNY
Yup. So this behemoth woman, this big fat lady working the cash register approaches the kid-

Carlo overdoes it with his fat woman impersonation:

CARLO
Hey. You lost, lil' boy? Huh?

FANNY
And Jason - I named the lil' boy Jason after my favorite Voorhees, though he's far from a serial killer - kid's a sweetheart-

CARLO
Wouldn't harm a FLY, Fred!

Fred nods, drinks.

FANNY
She leans down to Jason and says-

CARLO
Y'gonna catch the comet tonight?

FANNY
She's one of these creepy stranger danger strangers.
(MORE)

FANNY (CONT'D)
His mom interrupts, buys him this cap gun, die cast metal Fred, I used to have one, and they're off!

CARLO
Beep-beep! That's them driving!

FANNY
Fred, you look like you'd rather be anywhere else!

FRED
Sorry, I get that this is a best-selling book, but I'm just- I don't-

FANNY
You don't like it.

CARLO
YOU DON'T LIKE IT!?

FANNY
It's okay, Carlo.

CARLO
WHAT'S NOT TO LIKE!

FANNY
It's okay, Carlo.

CARLO
WE HAVEN'T EVEN GOT INTO IT, YET.

FANNY
It's okay, Carlo. I mean, he's right, but.

CARLO
THERE ARE LITERALLY ZOMBIES.

FANNY
Spoiler alert! Okay, let's not-abridged version for Fred, Fred with the little cokey meltdown.

FRED
I'm not having a meltdown, I'm- Yeah, I'm not quite uh. I'm sure it's *good*, but hard to tell with the, uh. Because, uh. Drugs.

FANNY
Like I said, abridged. Version. For FREDDY POO. Buddy approaches this blood-soaked little girl.

CARLO
Her skin's all BLEGH and she tries to KILL him, Fred! A LITTLE CHILD.

Carlo throws his arms up like he's never KNOWN such a thing.

CARLO (CONT'D)
It's good. It's so *effing good.* He's like *"You okay?"* and she's like-

SNAP! Fanny and Carlo *BITE and SNARL* at Fred! Doing their best zombie shriek.

CARLO (CONT'D)
RAAHAHCHHFGHGHGHHH!!!! There's blood ALL over her six year old face, god dammit!

FRED
Jesus! Take it easy. I get it. You're a zombie. Shit. Just take it easy with the screaming. Sorry, I'm- I'm LISTENING, but. Sensitive. Coke.

CARLO
She is *INFECTEEEDDD.* What else.

FANNY
He runs all like *WHAT. THE FUCK. IS GOING ON?!* Meanwhile mom and Jason get to their cabin and there's all this taxidermy, a big moose on the wall like-

Fanny does a "stuffed moose" pose.

FANNY (CONT'D)
Jason LOVES it. Poor kiddo doesn't have many friends, but he's got his mama. There's something about his mother that gives him the courage to explore this creepy, elaborate place which gets into a whole thematic message- FRED! Stay in it. Fred? Stay in it?

Fred drinks and nods a lot.

Carlo - officially Fanny's hype man - improvises bad sound effects as they "narrate."

FANNY (CONT'D)
Jason watches scary movies while mom makes birthday brownies for dad who's supposed to show that night.

CARLO
If only they knew!

FANNY
IF ONLY THEY KNEW there was a deadly outbreak. Something airborne. Something sinister, only affecting *WOMEN*...

FANNY (CONT'D)
Blah blah blah we gotta keep Fred awake. What else-

CARLO
THE BUS! There's a bus with a buncha dead people in it and they're all men, also!

FANNY
WELL DONE! Buddy hears this horn, this *"EEEEEEEeeeeEE."*

HEAR: the gradual volume of a BUS HORN **builds** and **builds.**

CARLO
(yelling)
BUDDY LOOKS THROUGH THE DOOR LIKE, OH SHIT! A DEAD BUS DRIVER!

FANNY
HUNCHED OVER THE WHEEL!

CARLO
HE PULLS HIS HEAD BACK!

Carlo assumes the role of DEAD BUS DRIVER. Fanny pulls him off an imaginary STEERING WHEEL.

CARLO (CONT'D)
And a bunch of scary shit happens-

FANNY
Like I said, abridged version-
Jason and his mom have NO fucking idea what's going on outside the safe bubble of their lil' cabin with the taxidermy moose.

Carlo and Fanny each freeze, "doing MOOSE EARS".

CARLO
WAIT WAIT WAIT WAIT. We left out the abandoned elementary school - that's scary ass SHIT! This strange dude takes Buddy fuckin' HOSTAGE and brings him to this elementary school.

FANNY
There's all these people held up in there, kind of my Dawn of the Dead homage, this old lady's sick, Buddy has a gun

CARLO
Buddy's got a piece on him. A .22 or some shit. Pulls it out and-

BANG! BANG! BANG! GUNSHOTS as Carlo and Fanny mime **shooting several invisible zombies** in the house (including FRED).

CARLO (CONT'D)
Blows EVERYBODY's brains out. He's a good shot. It's all self defense so it's like. COOL. But it's also like, *"UM. OH-KAY."*

Fanny jumps on Carlo's back for no reason. He gives her a PIGGY BACK RIDE for as long as he can:

FANNY
Anyway, shit's weird. I do a really good job of setting up this unsettling *world.*

CARLO
It's amazing.

FRED
Amazing.

CARLO
Stay in it, Fred!

FANNY
Yup. Storm clouds. A mysterious scent in the air.

CARLO
Phone line's dead. Mom and Jason can't get in touch with dad or the authorities or the cops or sorry I gotta put you down my back, ow.

Fanny drops off Carlo's back and RUNS AWAY.

CARLO (CONT'D)
That's when they hear a knock!

KNOCK KNOCK KNOCK! Fred and Carlo *SCREAM!*

It's Fanny - OUTSIDE - waving.

FANNY
It's just me! Great timing, right?!

Fred and Carlo nod.

Fanny runs like a spaz around the side of the house and through the back door, a little out of breath. Fanny uses the door as she pleases to switch roles between Mom and Buddy:

FANNY (CONT'D)
Mom answers the door. It's Buddy. *Can I help you?* And Jason peeks in from the next room.

CARLO
He's so freaked out by strangers and new people, but it's like. *MOMMY'll handle him. NOT!*

FANNY
She lets him in. I mean. He's handsome. He doesn't make a phone call. He DOES pull a blade on mom.

CLICK. Carlo brandishes an invisible SWITCHBLADE.

CARLO
Are you one of them? Hm?

FANNY
-Jason pulls his TOY GUN on Buddy.

She pretends to point an INVISIBLE GUN at Carlo.

CARLO
Heh. What're you gonna do with that, kid? Play Cops n' Robbers?

FANNY
Take whatever you want. Just please don't hurt my son. Mom thinks fast! Pulls a CLEAVER from the knife block, but Buddy's *FASTER.*

Carlo SWINGS, (pretend) HITS FANNY. She falls to the floor, into a TOP SHOT, laying on her back:

FANNY (CONT'D)
(peeking from the floor)
She's knocked out COLD. All Jason can see are her legs.

CARLO (O.S.)
Then somethin' REAL weird happens.

Fanny - as mom - shakes her legs from behind the KITCHEN ISLAND.

CARLO (O.S.) (CONT'D)
Is she having a seizure?

FANNY
And she's like *RUN! JASON RUN!*

CARLO
BUT BUDDY GOES AFTER HIM! It's SCARY because it's like IS THIS WHITE MAN WE TRUSTED GOING TO KILL THIS KID!?

Carlo chases Fanny around the living room. It's ridiculous.

FRED
This is ridiculous.

CARLO
Jason's hiding under the bed, clutching his mouth, trying not to make a sound. Then - all of a sudden - *MOM APPEARS. CHANGED!*

FANNY RISES FROM BEHIND THE COUCH! She has FANGS!

A SCARY ORCHESTRAL STING! There's that magical realism at work - her story is *landing*.

FRED
So mom turns into a zombie vampire?

The music STOPS on a dime. Fanny and Carlo break character.

FANNY
It's never explained what they are.

CARLO
Never gets explained.

CARLO (CONT'D)
That's what I love about it.

FANNY
Again, leaving out some deets, because cokey meltdown, so. Abridged. But *VENUS* isn't just about a zombie-like outbreak that only affects women. It's about gender politics.

FRED
I don't see it.

Carlo laughs (he *does* get it). Fred bristles.

FANNY
It's about how men cling to their mothers. These "invincible", infallible human beings who can do no wrong.

CARLO
I used to get mad at my mom when it was raining because I was like "You can control the weather, make it stop." I still think she can.

FRED
How's it end?

FANNY
Jason makes a run for it as Buddy is surrounded by The Infected emerging from the woods and they devour him alive, literally ripping out his heart and eating it.

CARLO
There's this part that, well you didn't get it because you didn't read it yet Fred but there's a thing like, Buddy *may* have done something fucked up to his ex, so he deserves it.

FANNY
The last pages have little Jason aimlessly wandering the country road in the dark, thick mist, heading into the mouth of the beast essentially, and then- headlights.

CARLO
It's his dad!

FANNY
I want you to feel like *Oh YES! It's DAD! The kid's SAVED!* Euphoric feelings of rescue aside, reality is, without the love and guidance of the great woman of his life, kid's never going to be himself again. Nothing beats the comfort and strength of our mothers.

CARLO
Our *MOTHERS*, Fred!

Carlo and Fanny crawl over the couch and pour DRINKS.

FRED
I dunno, my mom was kind of a bitch.

CARLO
Wow. Wow. Wow. Okay.

FANNY
On that note.

Fanny pours herself another glass of wine and takes a slice.

FANNY (CONT'D)
I just wanna take a sec to acknowledge my INCREDIBLE, my *ENTHUSIASTIC*, my *VERY WILLING* storytelling partner in scares, Mr. Carlo- What's your last name?

CARLO
Oh that's cool, I don't tell many people.

FANNY
Right on. The enigmatic MR. CARLO! Let's hear it!

Fanny applauds. Carlo joins.

Fred snaps his fingers. He is <u>not</u> sober.

22 INT. CABIN - CONTINUOUS - "**SATAN SINGER**" 22

CARLO
Fred, are you gonna go, or?

FRED
Like leave, or? (beat) OH! Yeah.
How 'bout something a lil' cheery.
All these tales of tortured kids.
How 'bout some music?

FANNY
Fred! That's a good idea! Wow!

Fred shoots her a boozy frown.

FANNY (CONT'D)
Truly! You're onto something. A
story about a SINGER.

FRED
What else.

CARLO
A singer... that's also a teen
slasher?

FANNY
Teen slasher singer.

FRED
A singer possessed by the devil.

FANNY
FRED YOU'RE ON A ROLL, BUDDY. A
singer. Her band. The devil?

CARLO
So fuckin' epic already!

Fred salutes with his beer and burps.

FRED
Yeah, there's something about her.
A quiet gal who always wanted to be
more. She'd do anything to sing on
national TV.

CARLO
It's like *A STAR IS BORN* but SATAN!

FANNY
And she's got this song. It's good. It's actually good.

FRED
And this is a BIG show. Millions of people watching.

CARLO
She's gonna be on American Idol.

FANNY
THAT'S STELLAR, DUDE. YES, CARLO! STAKES, CARLO! STAKES!

CARLO
(no idea what stakes are)
STAKES!

FANNY
I would sell my SOUL to sing on American Idol. Or a similar show that won't get us into copyright, um. Issues.

Fanny looks at us for a split second.

FANNY (CONT'D)
For the purposes of OUR story it's-

CARLO
The Big Talent Show. Live!

FRED
The Big Talent Show, Live!

FANNY
The Big Talent Show, Live!

CARLO
The Big Talent Show, LIVE!

Carlo accidentally kicks something over and quickly sits it back up.

CARLO (CONT'D)
And the singer, she's got a SHITTY boyfriend who really brings her down and probably doesn't want her to succeed.

FANNY
LOVE that detail Carlo, VERY relevant and well-articulated, sir! What's this vile boyfriend's name, Carlo?

CARLO
Uh. Carl?

FANNY
So close to Carlo.

FRED
That's great.

FRED (CONT'D)
She has one shot to make it happen but little does she know, the Devil's got a trick up his sleeve.

FANNY
Nothing's ever straight with Satan. Do your best "Devil" Fred. C'mon.

FRED
Nah.

FANNY
Make him interesting, too. The Devil takes many forms. Do the Devil as a bird or some shit.

FRED
I'm good.

CARLO
Wait, what!? I wanna see your devil bird! Fred, I wanna see that!

FANNY
Dude, Fred is like, talented.

Despite the context, this lands with Fred.

CARLO
Yeah?! You can't tell, but!

FANNY
Oh, he's good. HUMOR US, FRED.

Fred shakes his head and drinks more.

CARLO
You're shy!

FRED
Okay! A Devil bird. Shit.

Fred drunkenly "perches" on the arm of the couch.

FRED (CONT'D)
SQUAWK wanna be famous SQUAWK! No problem SQUAWK I'm the DEVIL.

Awkward pause. Fanny continues:

FANNY
Leading up to the big performance, the singer - Beth? Beth. Beth's got a sore throat. She's been talking to herself. Her skin's peeling. Everyone's like:

FRED
Hey. You okay?

CARLO
You don't look so good.

Fanny scratches herself, hinting at impending possession:

FANNY
Oh, I'm fine guys, let's KILL IT tonight.

Fanny coughs and gags.

As she SINGS, we hear a **HINT OF MUSICAL ACCOMPANIMENT:**

FANNY (CONT'D)
Especially funny as she's practicing her song. *La-de-dahhh feel the music, feel the light. La-de-daaahh everyone feel the music, feel the li-COUGHCOUGHCOUGH!*

FRED
Her bandmates are all nervous because it's like, SHE'S GONNA FUCK THIS UP FOR US. So she goes on American, uh- The Big Talent Show, Live.

Fanny HEADS TO THE KITCHEN:

FANNY
Beth reassures her band, her voice hoarse as hell, *Everything's gonna be fine. We're gonna rock n' roll. What's wrong with me?*

STAY ON FANNY as the LIGHTS DIM. The living room behind her feels like a **STAGE**. It feels like we're BACKSTAGE with Fanny.

HEAR - a bustling CROWD FILING IN TO THEIR SEATS.

Fanny turns to a VANITY, suspended in space.

FANNY (CONT'D)
Something doesn't feel right.

REVERSE: Fred is **SILHOUETTED** as THE DEVIL, his voice PITCHED LOW and unsettling (like Freddy Krueger).

FRED
FEELING A LITTLE UNDER THE WEATHER?

FANNY
Hey. I gave you my soul to be here. Don't fuck this up for me, Satan.

FRED
WOULDN'T DREAM OF IT.

Fanny SPASMS, SMASHING the UNSEEN VANITY MIRROR. We hear INVISIBLE GLASS SHATTERING.

CARLO (O.S.)
"Five minutes, Mrs. Walker!"

HEAR - A MUSICAL HORROR STING!

Carlo LOOKS AROUND THE ROOM as if he heard something.

CARLO (CONT'D)
Here come those STAKES!

Carlo does a pretty good "heartbeat" noise with his throat.

As Carlo announces her, his voice is AMPLIFIED as if through the walls of Madison Square Garden.

Fanny *SLAPS HERSELF*, trying to keep the evil in her at bay.

CARLO (CONT'D)
"Welcome to a nationally televised show that millions of people are watching! Hope nothing bad happens!

FANNY
(harsh whisper)
Hey. HEY. Don't fuck this up for me, The Devil!

FRED
BREAK LITERALLY ALL YOUR LIMBS OUT THERE, SWEETPEA.

CARLO
Ladies and gentlemen... what's her name again?

FANNY
We've been calling her Beth.

CARLO
OK PLEASE WELCOME BETH!

HEAR: THUNDEROUS APPLAUSE as Fanny approaches the mic - twitching, sweating, *staving inevitable evil...*

FANNY
This. Is an original.

LIGHTS DIM. The "crowd" falls silent.

She taps the mic. HEAR - imaginary MIC FEEDBACK.

This is the most atmospheric we've felt a story...

HEAR - A MASSIVE AUDIENCE CLAP and FADE TO WHISPERS.

Fanny **SINGS A SONG** that starts epic...

We CIRCLE FANNY, blinded by a powerful SPOTLIGHT.

Carlo sits next to Fred and does his best "British Talent Judge" voice.

CARLO
Absolutely phenomenal range. Wow.

FRED
Hell yeah. Agreed.

FANNY
...she continues singing... but then... she's not herself. *The lyrics turn HORRIFIC AND VIOLENT.*

THE MUSIC SWELLS! Fanny's singing oscillates between sweet and Satanic:

FANNY (CONT'D)
Kill all your mothers. Kill all your children and kill yoursssellvesss.

She continues singing, now *FULL DEVIL:*

FANNY (CONT'D)
GET READY FOR SOME SERIOUS EVIL. GET READY FOR SOME SERIOUS EVIL.LIKE I SAID, KILL ALL YOUR CHILDREN. KILL EACH OTHER. KILL YOURSELVVVVESSSSSS.

DANCE BREAK! Carlo, Fred, and Fanny execute a killer, SYNCHRONIZED DANCE. (Like - dare I say - *Ex-Machina*).

The room is now AWASH in DEVILISH RED LIGHT.

FANNY / CARLO / FRED
GET READY FOR SOME SERIOUS EVIL.
GET READY FOR SOME SERIOUS EVIL.
GET READY FOR SOME SERIOUS EVIL.
GET READY FOR THAT SERIOUS KAaAAeRG-

FANNY
SHE BARFS EVERYWHERE! Like, all over Madison Square Garden-level barf! Just five fuckin' minutes of straight barfing!

Fanny pretends to BARF.

The SOUND DESIGN is so visceral and *so fucking good* we practically *feel* THICK, WET VOMIT - *EVERYWHERE.*

CAMERA PANS around the room - to the walls and corners - as the unseen SHRIEK of the AUDIENCE in STADIUM SEATING grows DEAFENING (*"Oh my god! OH MY GOD! EW! WHAT THE HELL!"* etc.)

Fred and Carlo each stand up into spooky BACKLIT SINGLES:

CARLO
What in bloody hell is HAPPENING!?

FRED
OH GOD MAKE IT STOP! It's devil barf! It's burning!

Fanny continues to "barf". Then - breaking character:

FANNY
Then - a moment of respite.

The LIGHTING CHANGES - it's friendlier, somehow.

FANNY (CONT'D)
The audience stares in slack-jawed shock. Everyone, even Beth's shitty boyfriend is *covered* in Devil *barf.*

FRED
That's when he speaks through her!
I HOPE YOU ENJOYED THE SHOWWWW! BUT THE FUN'S JUST BEGUNNNN!

HELLISH LIGHT returns! CAMERA GOES *DUTCH.*

CARLO
Satan rips through her chest with his Devil arm!
(MORE)

CARLO (CONT'D)
It's like *Alien* but with a thrashing ELECTRIC GUITAR soundtrack! Thrashing SO hard?!

PROFILE ON FANNY as Fred's arm "drives through" Fanny - really just an optical illusion backlit and VERY FOGGY.

FANNY
I was gonna say, maybe he delivers a meaningful monologue on national television. Commentary on a toxic industry taking advantage of young, uh- talent.

SMASH TO REALITY - scene returns to normal.

FRED
Or sends his evil through TVs across America, possessing the country.

FANNY
We've seen that before.

CARLO
They did that in *Batman Forever.*

FRED
That wasn't the devil, though...

Carlo checks his PIZZA watch.

CARLO
Crap, I gotta go.

FANNY
NO! Carlo!! Pizza Man of the Year! Storytelling-Award-Winning Pizza Man Carlo! Why!?

FRED
That was Jim Carrey's Riddler. It couldn't be more different.

CARLO
Yeah, I got a cold Hawaiian that should've been in Wappingers Falls like 2 hours ago.

Carlo hops to his feet and <u>does a bad Michael Jackson spin</u>, pointing "gun fingers" at his new best friends.

CARLO (CONT'D)
Have a good night you guys.

FRED
It was Jim Carrey's
Riddler...

FANNY
We'll never forget you,
Scarecrow.

CARLO
It's one of those nights like - you *leave* to deliver a large pizza and end up doing blow and telling ghost stories, y'know? Heh. HEY, Fanny, could I... get your autograph?

FANNY
I mean. My pleasure.

23 EXT. FRED'S CABIN - CONTINUOUS 23

Carlo shuts the door to his car in the foreground, approaching Fanny with a PIZZA BOX. She signs it. Fred ogles.

CARLO
If you could write, *"To Carlo, thanks for telling ghost stories and doing coke"* or I dunno I'm not the writer or whatever.

FANNY
That's exactly what I wrote.

CARLO
You're the best. Well. 'Night.

Carlo hugs Fanny, then Fred, who taps him on the back like *"That's good. Done now."*

Carlo drives off, leaving his new best friends standing silhouetted in the doorway of the cabin.

Fanny grabs a BUCKET sitting on the porch and heads into the WOODS.

FRED
Where are you going?

FANNY
Gotta fill a bucket to take a much-needed cocaine *defa-cashe.* (beat) The plumbing is, uh. Yeah.

As Fanny leaves, we TRUCK-IN toward Fred's silhouette.

INSIDIOUS MUSIC SWELLS...

24 EXT. THE STREAM BEHIND FRED'S CABIN - NIGHT 24

The rain has stopped. HEAR the last groan of distant THUNDER.

Fanny fills a BUCKET with creek water.

She looks toward the house, FLICKERING FIRELIGHT within.

She can vaguely make out Fred's silhouette inside. She smiles. *Ah, new buddy Freddy...*

25 INT. FRED'S CABIN - MOMENTS LATER 25

Fanny enters with a heavy bucket of water.

FANNY
POTTY TIME!

STAY ON Fred throughout the following. He sits at the TABLE.

Fanny crosses frame and enters the bathroom, humming *"GET READY FOR SOME SERIOUS EVIL."*

We hear water slosh into the toilet.

The toilet FLUSHES.

Fanny enters the room, landing in her OTS:

FANNY (CONT'D)
Hey, so. I'm tired. I think I'm gonna head back.

She pours herself the last of the wine.

FANNY (CONT'D)
Why the long face? 'Cuz it's all over?

Fred does look... bummed. He is very **drunk**.

FRED
Hey, Fanny. For real. Thank you.

FANNY
For what?

FRED
I feel like I had fun for the first time in, uh- I needed this, is all.

FANNY
Let's "do coffee" before you head wherever you're going tomorrow.

Fred nods. Fanny starts to lea-

FRED
Wait.

She turns.

FRED (CONT'D)
I got one more.

FANNY
What. Story? Oh man, I'm-

FRED
Thought of it while you were out.

FANNY
It's four o'clock in the morning and I smell like cheese and campfire. You're. Definitely not drunk. But I can't resist a good tale. Gimme a logline.

FRED
I guess you'd call it a psychological thriller...?

FANNY
Always satisfying.

FRED
Right? About a killer and the woman who got under his skinnnnn.

FANNY
(yawning)
Truly Lifetime. I AM invested. Go.

FRED
Okay, so, she's this hard worker, you know? Bit of an ass kisser. Probably got endless support from mommy and daddy no matter how much she fucked up. Didn't have many *boyfriends,* but she had everything else a human being could've wanted. Cash. Opportunity. Privilege. Moved to the big city. Gets successful like. Instantly. She's one of those lucky "freaks" that just have. It.
(MORE)

FRED (CONT'D)
EASY. You know? Easy life. She does what she wants. Pisses- pisses him off.

FANNY
Classic tale of a boy emasculated by a powerful woman. What's it called? *The Life of Me: A Story of All Women Everywhere?*

FRED
His personal life wasn't so hot. He tried. Like. Really, REALLY tried. But he just- He didn't have-

FANNY
Talent?

FRED
No. He didn't have *"the fire."* The *FIRE*. Y'know?

FANNY
Too busy killing all the cats and dogs in the neighborhood, obvs.

FRED
Imagine writing copy for paint shops and chicken wing chains and you just wanna fuckin' kill someone. But you can't. Because it's wrong.

FANNY
Is this the story still?

FRED
Obvs. So, by total chance, he meets-

FANNY
This powerful woman who had it easy?

FRED
They actually hit it off, actually. She surprises him, She's a character, but for a hot sec, he thinks, *SHIT, I'M HAVING FUN*. Here's this... successful *weirdo* who just *brings it outta him*, you know? And for a second, it's like. *I forget- HE* forgets he's a killer.

Fanny eyes her NOTEBOOK on the table. It's been opened.

FRED (CONT'D)
He forgets about his screwed up life. He forgets he cheated on his wife. Forgets he lost his temper one two three many times. Forgets writing her all those *"mean letters."* This quirky little girl, she makes this creepy little killer feel... *Good!*

FANNY
I gotta admit, Fred. You're losing me.

FRED
I get it. You're a better storyteller than me. No no no. You're a BETTER STORYTELLER THAN ME! You're BETTER!

TRUCK-IN on Fanny, blood draining from her face.

FRED (CONT'D)
I'm just gonna jump to the end. It's good! Blah, blah, blah, they meet by this beautiful coincidence, make small talk on the road, only for one thing to lead to another: they decide to stay up all night and tell scary stories.

Fanny shifts her weight.

FRED (CONT'D)
It was her crazy idea. And the guy - sorry - the *KILLER* - he *LOVES* every second. 'Cuz he *LOVES* stories. But he sniffs her out like he sniffs out all the other, uh. *Humans.* Throughout the night, the fun kinda... Dies. His initial feeling of being included sort of falls away and he starts to feel used, like a *wind up monkey*. There to make this chick feel good about herself. First he felt SO inspired by her, but by the end of the night, he couldn't help but feel. *Used.*

FANNY
Fred.

FRED
Hm?

FANNY
What are you doing with that poker.

REVEAL: Fred is nervously brandishing the FIRE POKER.

FRED
Here *HE IS* making uh honest effort. Struggling. Spending his savings to tear away from a trash life to give *HIS* dream a shot. And she just gets to live hers. No problem.

FANNY
Okay, Fred, I get it. You read my notebook!

FRED
No. It's *MY* notebook. And I'm gonna tell you why. BECAUSE. It's. All. About. *ME.*

FANNY
That is my private shit. And, dude. If you're trying to scare me, it's not working. In fact, you're just starting to PISS ME OFF.

A beat of staring daggers.

FRED
This is about when those eerie *strings* kick in. Can you hear 'em? *REEE-oooo-WEEEEoOOOOoooooo...*

FANNY
No, Fred, I can't hear 'em because we're done. We're done telling stories and it's BEDTIME, man. Gimme my notebook.

FRED
Your notebook. With all your big ideas? Ten pages of which are about the *entitled WANNABE ACTOR and "LAME-O" WRITER?* A lonely, *EMASCULATED CREEP?* When did you write this? When you were sitting across from me eating pizza with your new best friend?!

FANNY
Well, shit, Fred, If I knew dairy turned you into a psycho I wouldn't have ordered you a pizza.

FRED
I paid for it.

Off Fanny:

FRED (CONT'D)
You've been taking notes. ALL NIGHT. All of *MY STORIES* are in here, Fanny. Why?

FANNY
Why are you taking this personally? THEY'RE OBSERVATIONS, FRED. OBSERVATIONS. IT'S *MATERIAL. MAH-TEER-I-AL. I'M THE WRITER. THE WRI-TER. I'M DOING THE WORK.* What are you doing? Renting a cabin, pretending to do your werewolf movie? Fuck off. You wanna have my life, Fred? SHUT THE FUCK UP AND DO THE WORK.

FRED
Your "work." Your genius brain at work, stealing from a *lame-o.*

FANNY
Spare me. I been steam-rolled and ignored. Complimented NOT ONCE for my ideas, but PLENTY for my tits. *Pantsed* on credit for work I didn't give a fuck about. Believe me, I've gotten *LITTLE* worthwhile material from your spooky stories.

FRED
All night. *Encouraged* to put myself out on a limb. Expose myself. Act like an ass for a fucking stranger. *Two strangers.* Just when you think you can let your guard down, a stuck-up little girl uses you for... *inspiration.*

FANNY
Little girl.

FRED
Spent all night cheering me on only to belittle me.

FANNY
Christ, Fred. Quit playing the victim card and develop some insulation. I'm not using you.

FRED
What?

FANNY
You're not *inspiring* to me, dude. What research do you think I'm compiling? Story notes for *Who Wants To Be Alone with a Strange White Guy?* Who're you kidding? You know, I figured you out.

FRED
Did you.

FANNY
I did. You're not a sad, emasculated failure. *You're not that interesting*. You are a man who thinks he's good, but knows he'll never be *great*.

Fred blinks, lowering his gaze to the floor.

FANNY (CONT'D)
It's literally insane we're having this discussion, it's insane if you're taking this personally, it's INSANE YOU'RE HOLDING A FIRE POKER BECAUSE you're NOT SCARING ME! SORRY! Now gimme my FUCKING NOTEBOOK or *I'LL FUCKING KILL YOU.* It's bedtime, bitch.

She extends her open palm.

FRED
Yeah. Sorry. Here.

He picks up the notebook and hands it to h-

FRED (CONT'D)
Wait! Why make it that easy?

FANNY
For fuck's sake.

FRED
We've been playing make believe all night. Why don't I chase you. We can pretend we're in one more story. If you hide and I can't find you, I'll give your notebook back. But if I catch you-

Fred giggles. Fanny gives a pity laugh.

FANNY
Just gimme the notebook. Please? Fred, please?

Fred shrugs and hands Fanny the notebook. As she goes to grab it, he rears back the poker.

FRED
SIKE!

FANNY
Fred, what the fuck, man.

FRED
Ah, come on, you wanted me to scare you! I'm not gonna hurt you. For real. Or maybe I'll bash your brains in. *RUN! RUNNN! RUNNNNNN!*

Fanny doesn't think twice - she fucking RUNS FOR IT!

A SHRIEK of ORCHESTRAL HORROR STRINGS!

FRED CHASES HER. SHE YELPS, SPRINTING UP THE STAIRS!

FRED SLIPS ON THE CARPET, sending the poker into the next room. Fanny gains precious seconds as she disappears around the banister.

FRED (CONT'D)
OW! GODDAMN IT! Man down!

UPSTAIRS - Fanny ducks into a RANDOM BEDROOM - clutching her bum knee (*fuckin' thing!*) and slides UNDER THE BED.

HOLD ON FANNY as we hear Fred STOMP UP THE STAIRS, footsteps are slow and deliberate.

THUMP. THUMP. THUMP.

ON THE STAIRS - Fred underlights himself with the FLASHLIGHT.

He's got a small GASH on his brow from his fall.

FRED (CONT'D)
Oh Faaaannnyyyyy... you should see me right now. I look like a creep.

He takes two more steps.

FRED (CONT'D)
Spooky footsteps, right? Hang on. Lemme start again for effect.

He descends a few steps and re-starts, NARRATING his way up:

FRED (CONT'D)
THUMP. THUMP. THUMP.

UNDER THE BED - TRUCK-IN to Fanny, covering her mouth to prevent a whimper.

THUMP.

THUMP.

THUMP.

Fred's SHAPE fills the DARKENED DOORWAY - flashlight in one hand, poker in the other.

The light FRAMES Fred in an unsettling way.

FRED (CONT'D)
(whispers)
Jeez. This might be the scariest story all night. And it's mine. See. Aren't I talented?

ON FANNY - the BEAM of Fred's flashlight dances on the floor in front of Fanny like the searchlight at a prison.

FRED (CONT'D)
Wow, Fanny. I guess you win.

We hear Fred leave.

We're convinced of it anyway...

The fear in Fanny's face is intense. She trembles, sweating.

With PAINFUL slowness, Fanny attempts her escape.

The floor CREAKS UNDER HER as she inches out from under the bed.

She stands, breathing a sigh of relief in the dark.

THE POWER FLIPS ON!

We HEAR electricity surge through the bowels of the house.

FRED (O.S.) (CONT'D)
The power's back!

Fanny turns. *FRED'S BEHIND HER!* He CACKLES.

FRED (CONT'D)
Fanny, *WAIT!*

She FLIES down the stairs, Fred TEARING AFTER HER.

HEAR - someone takes a TERRIBLE FALL, followed by...

A HORRIBLE *CRUNCH*.

REVEAL: Fanny on elbows, facing the stairs.

FANNY
Oh my god, Fred.

REVEAL: Fred has IMPALED HIMSELF ON THE FIRE POKER, lodging himself in the stairwell like a pig on a spit.

Fanny carefully crawls backwards on her elbows.

After a shocked beat, Fanny manages to stand and pace, ENTERING AND EXITING FRAME while Fred's corpse lie motionless.

We hear Fanny STOKE THE FIRE off-screen to get out of her head.

FRED SLOWLY COMES TO, managing a bloody GURGLE.

Fanny re-enters frame.

FRED
Look what you did.

FANNY
I'm sorry-

FRED
I was just kidding. I was only kidding. You th-thief.

FANNY
Don't flatter yourself. Y-you fragile maniac. Fuck, Fred! *Fuck!*

She hits her CBD pen with a shaky hand.

Blood spills from Fred's wounds like a spigot, cascading the staircase in RED.

FRED
Hey. Psst. Can you f-finish me off?

Fanny shakes her head *"No."*

FRED (CONT'D)
C-c'mon. You can t-tell everybody it was self defense. I'm obviously not gonna tell anybody.

He laughs bloody spittle down his chin.

HOLD ON: Fred as Fanny leaves.

FUMBLING in the next room. She lifts something HEAVY.

Fanny returns, holding a THICK, JAGGED LOG.

FANNY
How about some spooky, soaring, *"you're about to die"* music?

Fred nods. Fanny starts.

FANNY (CONT'D)
EEeeeeeeEEEEEEeoooooo...

Fred and Fanny's creepy, a capella horror humming transitions to an epically spooky, soaring ORCHESTRA.

FRED
EEeeeeeeEEEEEEeooOooOOOOOOO...

She rears the log back, ready to bash Fred's brains in.

ANGLE ON: FANNY's FEET. The log DROPS to the floor as Fred bleeds out - soft focus - in the background.

She leaves.

CUT TO:

26 EXT. FRED'S CABIN - DAWN 26

SUPER WIDE - Fanny exits the house and briskly walks away.

Seconds later: BETTINA'S TAXI PULLS IN THE DRIVEWAY.

27 EXT. FRED'S CABIN - DRIVEWAY - CONTINUOUS 27

Bettina gets out of the taxi and knocks on the front door.

BETTINA
Hello?

She peeks into the house.

BETTINA (CONT'D)
Mr. Banks? It's Bettina! Your driver!

Bettina notices the door is AJAR.

She looks around, shrugs. She pushes it open.

CREEEAK.

BETTINA'S POV: the house in disarray.

She notices empty beer cans. Coke on the table. Broken glass.

BETTINA (CONT'D)
Somebody had a good time.

She enters the FIREPLACE ROOM. Looks around.

BETTINA (CONT'D)
Mr. Banks? Mr. Banks? Mr. Banks?

Nobody home.

She looks around, eyeing an uneaten slice of cold pizza. She picks it up (*coast is clear*) and takes a bite.

As Bettina turns to go, she stops. Something catches her eye.

ANGLE ON: FANNY'S NOTEBOOK on the ground.

Bettina reaches down and picks it up. Flips through pages.

Unbeknownst to her, Fred's body lay - SOFT FOCUS - still entangled in the STAIRCASE behind her.

She takes another bite of pizza.

She reads something and smiles.

BETTINA (CONT'D)
Huh.

SMASH TO:

CREDITS.

A SOARING ORCHESTRAL HORROR TRACK takes us to:

A POST CREDITS SCENE...

28 EXT. SMALL TOWN - DAY 28

A pleasant afternoon.

Townies saunter by, chatting, enjoying the scenery.

We CREEP IN toward a LOCAL BOOK STORE. An EMPLOYEE sets up a SANDWICH BOARD outside.

As we approach, the image becomes clearer. It's a POSTER:

"SCARE ME: Grandpas, Werewolves, and Other Spooky Stories"

Author: BETTINA SIECZKOWSKI.

TODAY!

We land on a PORTRAIT of Bettina's happy face.

She looks great.

As a healthy flurry of foot traffic enters the store, we

CUT TO:

BLACK.

CPSIA information can be obtained
at www.ICGtesting.com
Printed in the USA
FSHW021646081220